IMAGE AND SYMBOL IN THE SACRED POETRY

OF

RICHARD CRASHAW

IMAGE AND SYMBOL

IN THE

SACRED POETRY

OF

RICHARD CRASHAW

BY

GEORGE WALTON WILLIAMS

UNIVERSITY OF SOUTH CAROLINA PRESS
COLUMBIA, S. C.

Copyright © 1963 by the University of South Carolina Press

Library of Congress Catalog Card Number 63-12394

First Edition, 1963
Second Edition, 1967

Printed by The R. L. Bryan Company, Columbia, S. C.

TO MY PARENTS

PREFACE

THIS STUDY OFFERS a *catalogue raisonné* of the symbolic imagery in the sacred poetry of Richard Crashaw. It embodies the results of an intensive rather than extensive analysis of the sacred poems attempting to discover the breadth of meaning that the religious symbols had for Crashaw and to show how the several symbols and poems interrelate. The dissection will no doubt seem often supererogatory, for completeness has been thought desirable even at the risks of repetition and of explicating the obvious.

The basic text for the inquiry has been L. C. Martin's edition, *The Poems English Latin and Greek of Richard Crashaw* (Second Edition. Oxford: Clarendon Press, 1957). The method of reference should be explained. For short poems: after the page number a large Roman numeral indicates the position of the poem on the page; no titles are given. For long poems: after the page number a small Roman numeral indicates the stanza, Arabic numerals (preceded by l. or ll.) refer to lines; short titles are given.

Specific citations to the writings of Dionysius, St. Teresa, St. John of the Cross, Southwell, Donne, Herbert, and Vaughan are made (in brackets) to the standard editions. After a reference to the Book of Common Prayer, "etc." means "and later editions."

I have followed the printing conventions of the original editions (as found in Martin) though producing thereby an anomaly. The English printer of Crashaw's 1646 volume practiced modern stlying for *i, j, u, v*; the French printer of the 1652 volume practiced old styling. One change has been made: the italic type of the 1634 Latin collection and of a few English poems has been represented by roman.

The study was originally compiled as a master's thesis at the University of Virginia, *teneræ ætatis flores*. It has been revised and rewritten, but its scope and intent remain the same. I am indebted for considerable assistance to Professors Fredson Bowers and the late Dan Norton, the directors of the thesis. Mr. Bowers and Professor Cyrus Hoy have been good enough to read the final version; had I felt capable of following all their suggestions, the volume would have been worthier of their approval.

I acknowledge with thanks the support of Adger and DuPont Fellowships at the University of Virginia. I am grateful also to the Duke University Research Council for assistance in the preparation and publication of the manuscript and to the Society for College Work of the Episcopal Church for making possible a summer's study at the Episcopal Theological School, Cambridge. My thanks go as well to the industrious and indulgent staffs at the libraries of the University of Virginia, the Episcopal Theological School, Harvard University, and Duke University. In typing, Mrs. Charles Muller and Miss Dorothy Roberts have been particularly helpful.

Thanks finally to three patient people—Harriet, George, and Ellison.

August 21, 1962   G. W. W.
Duke University

Contents

I. The Poet-Saint and the Baroque

Richard Crashaw diffidently subtitled the two collections of his secular poems "Other Poems," and by that deliberate otherness set them apart from his principal work, subtitled "Sacred Poems." The best that could be said of the secular *Delights of the Muses* was that they were "as sweet as they [were] innocent." The sacred poems on the other hand were the *Steps to the Temple* by which and through which the reader was "to climbe heaven"; they were the *Carmen Deo Nostro* which aimed "to burne the hart with heauenly fire." Thus the *dulce* of the secular poems was as clearly marked as was the *utile* of the sacred poems; where the secular poems pleased merely, the sacred poems purposed no less than "to measure the soule into that better world."[1] In terms of high purpose, sacred poetry was the chief of the delights of the muse of Richard Crashaw.

The earliest poems of this "Poet and Saint" were translations of the Psalms; the earliest published poem was introductory to a volume of sermons. Crashaw's first printed book was his *Epigrammatum sacrorum liber,* published in Cambridge in 1634, a collection of his sacred epigrams in Latin; a second edition, enlarged, appeared in 1670. Other Latin religious epigrams, preserved in manuscripts, were published posthumously.[2] Most of his maturer religious poems, composed in English (some of them were translations of the epigrams), Crashaw published in two editions of his *Steps to the Temple* (London, 1646 and 1648), the second edition repeating the contents of the first and adding paraphrases of several medieval hymns. Many of the longer poems in the editions of 1646 and 1648, extensively revised before Crashaw's death in 1649, were posthumously published with the hymns as *Carmen Deo Nostro* (Paris, 1652) under the editorship of Thomas Car, Crashaw's friend. The volume included a poem to the Countess of Denbigh, a longer and much altered version of which was printed separately as *A Letter to the Countess of Denbigh* (1653?). These manuscripts and printed books constitute the corpus of Crashaw's sacred poetry.

[1] L. C. Martin, *The Poems English Latin and Greek of Richard Crashaw* (2nd edit., Oxford, 1957), pp. 147, 213; 73, 205, 231; 76, 235, 75. All quotations from Crashaw are taken from this text.

[2] In Alexander B. Grosart, *The Complete Works of Richard Crashaw* (London, 1872).

Many of the sources for the matter and manner of Crashaw's poetry, Crashaw mentions directly in the poetry. The obvious original is the Bible, and Crashaw seems to have read Hebrew, Greek, Latin, and English versions. Stimulated by his father, the eminent Puritan divine, Crashaw paraphrased Psalms 23 and 137 as perhaps his earliest works.[3] The *Epigrammata Sacra* are all (but one) based on the New Testament. Some of them probably derive from academic exercises at Charterhouse; some perhaps from an even earlier school. Most of them were written as a requirement of Crashaw's scholarship at Pembroke and are dated between 1631 and 1635.[4]

But even before the volume of 1634 was published, Crashaw had already made a reputation for himself as a poet. He came up to Cambridge in 1631 evidently known as a poet, for he was immediately preparing elegiac verses on the obsequies of eminent Cambridge figures. More tellingly, he had provided introductory poems for at least three highly respectable volumes by the date of the *Epigrammata Sacra*.[5] He therefore looked back from the relative maturity of 1634 to his *juvenilia*, the epigrams, as he wrote in the Dedication of the *Epigrammata* to Benjamin Lany:

> Ignoscas igitur (vir colendissime) properanti sub ora Apollinis sui, primæque adolescentiæ lascivia exultanti Musæ. Teneræ ætatis flores adfert, non fructus seræ.[6]
>
> [Forgive, then, most Reverend Sir, the Muse hastening into the presence of her Apollo, and exulting in the wantonness of earliest youth. She offers the flowers of a tender age, not the fruits of a late one.]

[3] Martin, pp. 435, xcii.

[4] Austin Warren, *Richard Crashaw A Study in Baroque Sensibility* (University, La., 1939), p. 22; Leicester Bradner, *Musae Anglicanae* (New York, 1940), pp. 2-4, 332-333. Sister Maris Stella Milhaupt has written a very serviceable dissertation translating the Latin epigrams and dating them: *The Latin Epigrams of Richard Crashaw with Translations, Commentary, and Notes* (Ann Arbor, Mich.: University Microfilms, Inc., 1964). She has demonstrated that the order of the epigrams in the edition of 1634 is the order of weekly composition from summer 1631 to May 1634 and that the Tanner MS. continues the sequence through January 1635.

[5] Martin, p. lxxxvii. These were Lancelot Andrewes' *XCVI Sermons* (1631 or 1632; see *TLS*, 21, 28 August 1937, pp. 608, 624); Henry Issacson's *Chronologie explained* (1633); Lessius' *Hygiasticon or the Right Course of Preserving Life and Health* (Cambridge, 1634). In addition, Crashaw composed commemorative verses for Samuel Brooke, Master of Trinity, died Sept. 16, 1631; John Mansel, President of Queens', died Oct. 7, 1631; William Herrys, Fellow of Pembroke (scholar of Christ's 1624-1631), died Oct. 15, 1631; Robert Heath, Chief Justice of Common Pleas, promoted Oct. 26, 1631; the Princess Mary, born Nov. 4, 1631. This extra-parietal reputation may have attracted the attention of another Cambridge poet, John Milton, scholar of Christ's until his graduation as M.A., July 3, 1632. Both poets presumably contributed memorial verses to the *Justa Edouardo King* (1637) (Martin, p. xcii); both poets composed character sketches of Satan in Hell, the earlier and inferior inspiring the later and greater (cf. note 25, p. 62).

[6] Martin, p. 6; the translation is from Grosart's edition.

Where the Bible supplied the substance for the epigrams, two Latin poets supplied the style. Crashaw acknowledges Catullus and Martial in his remarks "To the Reader." Though he laments their profane verses, he shows himself much influenced by their styles. Catullus' sparrow is not of a feather with David's swallow, nor do Martial's obscenities flock with Christian purity; but elements of Martial's style — pleasure in the paradox and the witty contradiction — permeate Crashaw's entire career and lend themselves naturally to a method expressive of the paradox of the Christian life. It is in the early collection that the influence of other elements of Martial's style is strongest and most effective. Here that influence demands brevity, succinctness, balance, and the sudden sharp turn of meaning concealed in the last words; above all else it demands intellectual control. It acts as a sort of check on Crashaw's exuberance.

Most of the stylistic devices that characterize the late poems occur in these youthful works; the only conspicuous trait that is lacking is abandon. This abandon, particularly in the constant shifting of metaphor, tends to mar some of the later and better known poems; the firmness of the early epigrams makes them structurally finer than the late diffuse exaltations. The finest lines Crashaw ever wrote offer a valuable exemplum here. They are the concluding lines to "The Flaming Heart"; Crashaw composed them between the publication of the 1648 version of the poem and his death in 1649. They are hence his latest and his maturest work.

> O thou vndanted daughter of desires!
> By all thy dowr of LIGHTS & FIRES;
> By all the eagle in thee, all the doue;
> By all thy liues & deaths of loue;
> By thy larg draughts of intellectuall day,
> And by thy thirsts of loue more large then they;
> By all thy brim-fill'd Bowles of feirce desire
> By thy last Morning's draught of liquid fire;
> By the full kingdome of that finall kisse
> That seiz'd thy parting Soul, & seal'd thee his;
> By all the heau'ns thou hast in him
> (Fair sister of the SERAPHIM!)
> By all of HIM we haue in THEE;
> Leaue nothing of my SELF in me.
> Let me so read thy life, that I
> Vnto all life of mine may dy.

The passage is generally described as typically Crashavian. It is enthusiastic, it soars exultingly, it is climactic, it seems to be all wing; but underneath are the everlasting forms of the Litany. The anaphora by its anticipation spurs on this Pegasus and by its recollection reins him in. The passage is an example of the good effect that discipline can exercise on even the most volatile temperament. Crashaw was not often able to command his pen so well when he became excited about his God or his religion. Had he remembered his youthful lessons in Martial he would have been not only "by far the greatest writer of the . . . sacred epigram in England"[7] but a poet ranking with the "best English lyric poets."[8] Something was lost when Crashaw gave up the order of the pagan poet for the ardor of the Christian saint.

The influence of John Donne was one of analysis and brain work. Donne's poems were published in 1633, and a revision between the 1646 and 1648 versions of "The Weeper" suggests that Crashaw had remembered Donne's "Twickenham Garden." The influence is, however, general rather than specific and is transmitted chiefly through the foremost successor in the Donne tradition, George Herbert.[9]

George Herbert's English devotional poems were posthumously published in 1633 as *The Temple;* Crashaw's second volume of poetry, *Steps to the Temple* (1646), was modestly named with Herbert's volume in mind. That Crashaw admired Herbert is clear from Crashaw's poem accompanying a copy of *The Temple* presented to a gentlewoman: "These white plumes of his . . . every day to heaven will send you."[10] That he did not follow Herbert's lead in matters of style is equally clear. Crashaw's "Charitas Nimia" and his "Song upon the Bleeding Crucifix" disclose an Herbertian tone and structure respectively; but they are a small company.

It is natural, almost necessary, to compare Crashaw with Herbert — "*Herbert's* second, but equall," as Crashaw's first editor termed him, thus establishing the tradition of this comparison.[11] Two elements in contrast deserve brief mention. In Herbert there is a close relationship between the established forms of the liturgy and the nice articulation of the poems.[12] Crashaw loved the beauty of holiness and the decency of that same liturgy every bit as much as Herbert, yet the architecture

[7] Bradner, p. 92.

[8] Joseph H. Summers, *George Herbert: His Religion and Art* (Cambridge, Mass., 1954), p. 11.

[9] *See* George Williamson, *The Donne Tradition* (Cambridge, Mass., 1930), p. 112.

[10] Martin, p. 130.

[11] *Ibid.,* p. 75, "Preface to the Reader"; the author is unknown.

[12] Summers, *passim.*

of the eucharist seldom informs the poetry. The resilience and the tough intellectuality of Donne and Herbert might have been admired by Crashaw but were not emulated. Herbert's erudition in faith and practice and particularly in typology is well known.[13] Crashaw, too, was a man of extensive learning and mental agility, yet his learning does not manifest itself in the poetry. Typology can convey extraordinarily rich connotations and levels of meaning, yet it is practically nonexistent in Crashaw's poetry. Crashaw's typological allusions occur generally in his translations; typology never seems to have become a part of his poetic imagination as it bountifully did of Herbert's.

What influence these two English poets had in the matter of analysis was in sharp contrast to another and more congenial spirit coming from the Continent. That spirit Crashaw could have read in two other English devotional poets, Robert Southwell and Giles Fletcher (though there is no sure evidence that he knew their works).

> Out of a sympathetic study of Southwell and Fletcher, Crashaw could, without question, have acquired the essentials of his final style: the antithesis, the oxymoron, the paradox, alliteration, homoioteleuton; sensuous metaphors for sensuous objects, the sensuous treatment of sacred themes. Assuredly, Crashaw must have read them both. But that in both predecessors which was akin to Crashaw had come to them from the Italian *concettists*.[14]

The work of the *concettists* had its most characteristic expression in the poetry of the cavalier Giambattista Marino. The anonymous author of the 'Preface' to *Steps to the Temple* remarks that Crashaw taught himself Italian and Spanish, and Crashaw's reaction to Italian poetry appears in his translations written before 1635 of some of Marino's sacred epigrams and secular songs.[15] Crashaw's interest is more conspicuous in his longest poem, the translation of Marino's "Sospetto d'Herode," the first canto of his *La Strage de gli Innocenti*.[16] Marino's poem contains a rich supply of metaphysical image and extravagant conceit; Crashaw's poems contains an even richer supply. Conduct, approval,

---

[13] Rosemund Tuve, *A Reading of George Herbert* (Chicago, 1952).

[14] Warren, *Richard Crashaw*, pp. 117-118.

[15] Mario Praz, *Richard Crashaw* (Brescia, 1945), pp. 144-145. The second half of this study, "L'Arte di Richard Crashaw," has been published in English translation in *The Flaming Heart: Essays on Crashaw, Machiavelli, and Other Studies in the Relations between Italian and English Literature from Chaucer to T. S. Eliot* (Garden City, N. Y., 1958) as "The Flaming Heart: Richard Crashaw and the Baroque," pp. 204-263; all citations will be to this translation: pp. 231-232.

[16] Praz, *Flaming Heart*, pp. 231-238. See Ruth Wallerstein, *Richard Crashaw A Study in Style and Poetic Development* (Madison, 1935), pp. 73-109.

and encouragement for his extravagances Crashaw would have received from his friend and fellow poet, Abraham Cowley, and from Edward Benlowes and John Cleveland.[17] But in adapting such conceits to religious themes in the vernacular Crashaw might well have felt himself lucky in having also the example of the Italian tradition and the sanction of the distinguished Italian cavalier before him.

St. Teresa of Jesus, of Avila, was the saint whom Crashaw chose as his patron. After a busy life of writing and administration, St. Teresa died in 1582. She was beatified in 1614 and canonized in 1622, and, thanks to her literary works, she soon became one of the most popular saints of the seventeenth century. She may have been brought to Crashaw's attention first in 1638 through the interest of Joseph Beaumont, a Fellow of Peterhouse; she certainly filled Crashaw's finest poetry and occupied his last poetic breath. That Crashaw read her books and admired her immensely is demonstrable from the poetic trilogy he wrote in her honor: "The Hymn to St. Teresa," "An Apology for the fore-going Hymn," and "The Flaming Heart." The most influential of the Saint's books was her autobiography, *Vida,* published in Spanish in 1588. It was first translated into English by William Malone and published in Antwerp in 1611. Another translation into English made by Sir Tobias Mathew and entitled *The Flaming Heart* was published in London in 1623; a second edition of this work appeared in Antwerp in 1642. No other of the Saint's works was translated into English in Crashaw's lifetime, but all her principal writings were available in the Spanish collected edition of 1588: *Avisos espirituales* [in part] (*Relations*), *Camino de Perfeccion* (*Way of Perfection*), *Castillo interior o las Moradas* (*Interior Castle*), and *Exclamaciones* (*Exclamations*). One opuscule, *Conceptos del amor de Dios* (*Conceptions of the Love of God*), appeared in 1611.[18] Crashaw thus could command editions of all of St. Teresa's devotional works; he must be believed when he says that he read them and took fire from them. He too had a flaming heart.

Crashaw mentions another mystic, Dionysius the Aeropagite. (The authenticity of Dionysius' writings need not be of concern here; the

[17] Laura Pettoello, "A Current Misconception Concerning the Influence of Marino's Poetry on Crashaw's," *MLR,* LII (July 1957), 327.

[18] E. Allison Peers, *The Complete Works of Saint Teresa of Jesus* (New York, 1946), I, xlviii-xlvi; III, 379-383, and *Studies of the Spanish Mystics* (London, 1927-1930), I, 437. Crashaw knew also the biography compiled by Francisco de Ribera, *Vida De Santa Teresa de Jesús* (Salamanca, 1590); he refers to it in a marginal note on a manuscript of "The Hymn to St. Teresa" (Martin, p. xciii). All quotations from St. Teresa's works are drawn from Peers' translation and edition except those from the *Life,* which are drawn from *The Flaming Heart* (1642).

year of composition and the identity of the writer do not affect the validity of the mystical experience. In the seventeenth century a commendably large and sound body of theological learning and commentary authenticated the mystic.) Crashaw was acquainted with the *Letters* and the *Treatise on Mystical Theology* at least, probably with the *On Divine Names* and the two books of *Hierarchies*. He was particularly impressed by the conversion of the author during the Crucifixion of Christ, and he referred to the episode in one of his poems.

Crashaw embraced the Roman Catholic faith between 1643 and 1646, but only "The Hymn in the Glorious Assumption of our Blessed Lady" in the volume of the latter year records a doctrine exclusively Roman. The second edition of *Steps to the Temple* (1648) added several other hymns of the medieval Church: "Vexilla Regis," "Stabat Mater Dolorosa," "Adoro Te," "Lauda Sion Salvatorem," "Dies Irae," and "O Gloriosa Domina."

From these sources, and from others which he mentions or does not mention, Crashaw drew his techniques, his content, and his inspiration; but their greatest contribution to his development as a poet lay in their transmitting to him the commonplace symbols of the Christian Church, traditional to European literature, theology, and philosophy from the time of the Middle Ages. And in bequeathing this legacy, they were not alone; Crashaw was influenced by many sources and forces he does not mention. The quotation in these pages from Crashaw's acknowledged sources therefore must be understood generally to represent not so much evidences of limited or direct dependence as examples of well-known and widespread custom, tradition, or learning. Crashaw's symbology was composed of commonplaces.

The attentive reader of Crashaw's poems notices at once the luxuriance of symbols and of symbolic imagery. The luxuriance depends on a rapid shifting of metaphors as one image glides into another. This rich flexibility of mixed metaphors should suggest that the words of the passage are not being used strictly or with their customary meanings. They are under the control of the "wit of love" and they are more often lovely than witty. The luxuriance depends also on the constant repetition of the same images. Words like "nest" and "breast," "flood" and "blood," "tomb" and "womb," "dart" and "heart," and many more reappear on every page. There are also adjectives — "soft," "sweet," "bright," "delicious," "fair" — which Crashaw employs so often that they seem quite to have lost their original specific referents. Such unnatural emphasis and obvious repetition suggest that Crashaw was using the terms with symbolic significance and that he had forgotten their standard definitions. Those who take offense at the usage of these repeated symbols are not forgetting (along with Crashaw) the meaning which they have at face value. This process of willful obliviscence may not be easy, may not be possible for some, but is essential to an appreciative study of the poetry. These "repeaters" control the tone of the imagery in the poetry and are in large part responsible for the integrity of the poems.

There would seem to be a certain sterility in the imagination that so repeats itself; at least, this repetition requires some justification. The justification, presumably, lies in the task, cheerfully assumed, of describing the indescribable. It is a task which confronts any poet who proposes to discuss the nature of God and the wonders of His love. And each poet responds to his challenge in his own manner: one wrestles, one analyzes, one adores.

The words which Crashaw uses most fondly, those he delights in, have gained new and in some cases private meanings for him. They become talismans of almost magical worth, and they are used generously because they are most effective when they can interact in image clusters. Common glosses on the individual appearances of the word are of secondary helpfulness, for the meaning of the talisman may be apprehended only after it has been examined in the round, with all its important occurrences considered. Then one may feel he has approached the larger interpretation of the poem and the understanding of the mind of the poet.

There are two considerations that bear on the significance of these talismans. The first is chronological development. Generally the images move from schoolboyish simplicity to a highly mature symbolic currency. Sometimes, however, Crashaw seems to have achieved in his earliest work what is almost complete comprehension of his later symbolic usage. At least, in the youthful epigrams, the poet reveals a cognizance of the exact potential of the image. The early images thus provide valuable material in understanding the late work. The second consideration is that of precision of use. Crashaw did not always use an image in the same careful sense. The question must be raised: how is the poet employing the symbol? Furthermore, in any use of the symbol there is sure to be some vagueness. This vagueness is, no doubt, intentional; it is unavoidable, indeed, when one is trying to express divinity. The poet cultivates this imprecision in order to manifest the divine to mortal eyes. The reverse of this process and its outcome — considered unfortunate by some readers — are seen in *Paradise Lost,* Book V, in Raphael's description of the war in heaven. Attempting to describe things beyond the reach of human comprehension "By lik'ning spiritual to corporeal forms, As may express them best" (ll. 573-574) gains for the reader a seventeenth-century war and loses him heaven. Rather than admit the frightful possibility of losing heaven for his readers, whom he intends to lift by his verse "some yards above the ground," [19] Crashaw relies on a method basically mystical in broadly interpreting the symbol as the vehicle of his meaning. The imagery Milton employs is sufficiently exact to provoke in the mind of the reader a picture of army maneuvers; the imagery in Crashaw is often generously vague and indeterminate. The technique of imagery is well defined by St. Bernard:

> For although the words by which these visions or similitudes are described seem to celebrate substances and corporal things, they are on the contrary, spiritual things which are therein ministered to us, and therefore their causes and reasons should also be sought for in the spirit.[20]

The repetition of words and images discloses another aspect of Crashaw's religious poetry. Each of the rhyming pairs mentioned earlier includes a part of the body. Each of the adjectives pertains to one of the senses. This repeated emphasis on the flesh is characteristic of the baroque, a style encouraged by the deliberations of the Council of Trent. The Council, "by sanctioning the veneration of images and by its emphasis upon transubstantiation . . . , gave the pious a confidence in sensory experience." [21] As a consequence, religious poetry of the sixteenth and seventeenth centuries began to admire and elaborate sensory experiences and sensory images, particularly those associated with the Passion. "Baroque piety and art are able to consolidate and fulfill experience at the level of the flesh, and they do so ardently, triumphantly, unthinkingly. If the image is sufficiently powerful, if the physical sensation is adequately enriched, . . . the act of faith can be performed and terminated, literally, in the senses." [22] To accomplish this experience, the image must be made powerful. Baroque strives to be a style of force; it convinces by overstatement, by exuberance, by superlative. It transcends the limits of traditional images and forms, refashioning them to break them with great energy or soaring above them on rhapsodic

---

[19] Martin, p. 75, "Preface to the Reader."

[20] Bernard, *Sermones in Cantica, Patrologia Latina*, Migne, CLXXXIII, 945, quoted in Stephen Manning, "The Meaning of 'The Weeper,' " *ELH*, XXII (March 1955), 34.

[21] Wylie Sypher, *Four Stages of Renaissance Style* (Garden City, N. Y., 1955), p. 187. I am much indebted to Mr. Sypher's insight in his third stage, "Baroque," pp. 180-251. Other relevant accounts occur in Warren, *Richard Crashaw*, pp. 63-193; Praz, *Flaming Heart*, pp. 204-263.

[22] Sypher, *loc. cit.*

wings. Crashaw's translations, by their extreme elaboration of their originals, and Crashaw's frequent attention to the concept of divine abundance, for example, manifest this overstatement.

Another quality of the baroque is redundance. Where one image will serve, Crashaw gives several; his repeated words and his clusters of mixed metaphors encrust the poem with an exterior which is shimmering and colorful. Such a covering seems always to be in motion, concealing an immense, dynamic vigor within. Movement and fluidity, or restlessness, similarly characterize the style; Crashaw's poetic imagination is constantly shifting from one sensory image to another. Power and movement combine to produce surprise. Crashaw intends to startle, and he achieves his intention by carrying his images just one step further in their development, so that the familiar is suddenly remarkable — even, sometimes, grotesque.

Baroque is tremendously vital and energetic, but there is a danger in this style that the poet will copy the gyration of the powerful line from the outside without having his line grow from its own necessary power within. Crashaw is perhaps subject to this defect, and the cause of the defect may lie in the fondness for those very sensory words and images already listed. Crashaw's favorite words are facile in coming to hand, and the rhymes that go along with them assist in writing the poem and in shaping the metaphoric shimmer and agitation. These repeated images have their symbolic meanings, but their proliferation constitutes a part of Crashaw's baroque sensibility. He uses his talismans to create enthusiasm and excess, to provide *copia,* to suggest restlessness, to astonish, but if the critic looks below and within he will not always find that intrinsic power and sturdiness to hold the experience together or to give it a formal or intellectual structure. The passage from "The Flaming Heart" comes to mind; there is power within and shimmer without, there is exultation intrinsic and extrinsic. But there are none of the favorite repetitions.

"Baroque piety and baroque art alike modified, or corrupted, the doctrine of transubstantiation; the flesh did not become spiritual — the spiritual became fleshly. . . . Then baroque art [changed] from a victorious exhibition of power to a gaudy display of self-assurance or self-satisfaction. . . . As soon as the art of . . . energetic strife (*agonistes*) is replaced . . . , the baroque image loses its full charge and becomes merely seductive or agreeable. . . . When the baroque imagination fails in power, Counter-Reformation art decays to . . . prettiness, and sentimentality." [23] Crashaw is not always exempt from this decay.

[23] *Ibid.,* pp. 188, 242-243.

The chapters which follow demonstrate how Crashaw treated the religious commonplace, both specific symbols and what may be called general symbols or symbolic concepts. Of this second type there are perhaps three. These are closely interrelated and pervade the poetry with a consistency which would appear to be peculiarly Crashavian. The first of these is the symbolic concept of quantity (Chapter II). God's greatness is seen as exceedingly abundant and as exceedingly small; in comparison to this greatness man is an insignificant nothing. The second symbolic concept is that of color (Chapters III, IV). Crashaw sees the love of God represented in many shades of white and red. Paradoxically, the sinfulness of man is also red, as his purity and penitence are white. The love of God is at the same time a shining light illuminating the darkness of this world and the deep blackness of man's sinfulness. The third symbolic concept, liquidity (Chapter V), secures its most meaningful effects in combining with the other two; so it reflects the quantities of God in floods and drops, His colors in tears and blood, water and wine. The mechanical classification of the symbols is artificial and, no doubt, violently opposed to Crashaw's poetic intention and integrity, but classification was essential. To obviate some of the disadvantages of the system, frequent cross references call attention to the fact that the art of the poet is one.

Abraham Cowley termed Crashaw "Poet and Saint." Crashaw's sacred poems reveal the justness of this happy phrase most clearly in their use of the symbols and symbolic concepts. The examination of these symbolic significances will tend to clarify the interweaving of poetry and saintliness and to demonstrate Crashaw's ability to marry a poetic image and a powerful sacred connotation and to make the two live together peaceably, congenially, and in a manner mutually co-operative. Among a very few English poets Crashaw has succeeded often in being simultaneously poet and saint.

II. Quantity

THE CONCEPT of quantity is basic to Crashaw's poetry. It underlies in one way or another poems early and late, and it constitutes for Crashaw perhaps the readiest method of praise. The most conspicuous — and most baroque—aspect of quantity is abundance; God's plenty is found in the poetry, as in Nature, everywhere. But God is to be admired not only in extension but in contraction also; Crashaw discovers infinite riches in little rooms. His baroque spirit sets up highly restricted limits and confines and then bursts through them magnificently.[1] God's abundant majesty in greatness and smallness ought to be praised, but man should consider his significance in comparison with that majesty. God's abundance, God's infinitesimalness, and man's insignificance are the three symbolic approaches by which Crashaw attempts to express the quantities of God.

1. Abundance

Some of the most striking symbols in Crashaw's poetry represent the abundance and supreme generosity of God. The source of these symbols lies in the primordium of the Judaeo-Christian cosmogony. God fulfills Himself most completely in His creative giving throughout the Bible; but this is evidenced first in Genesis in the creation of the world. The generosity of the creative gift effects the astonishing copiousness and complexity of the *liber creaturarum*. The abundance of this creation is paralleled by an abundance of destruction. The Noachic Deluge (Genesis 7) offers a second example of the amplitude of God's power and majesty. But the abundance bears a symbolic interpretation even here. For the flood is, like the fortunate fall, a paradoxical opportunity for the Divine Being to show His grace through the death of the corrupt members of the race and the election of a single family to preservation on earth. Both the creation and the flood are more than simple functions of abundance; they are also indications of good and grace. The unlimited variety and number of created beings and the over-

---

[1] Sypher, *Four Stages of Renaissance Style*, pp. 184, 212.

whelming immensity of the flood multiply the virtues of goodness and grace to an infinite power.[2]

The virtues of abundance thus established in the foundation of the world are exalted everywhere in the Scriptures — the Psalmist sings: "I will sing unto the Lord, because he hath dealt bountifully with me" (Ps. 13.6) — but the concept finds its complete manifestation in the act of supreme generosity and abundant giving in the gift of His Son by God the Father. Christ complements this act of utmost generosity and bounty by sacrificially giving Himself in return. The bounty in the life and death of Christ caught the devout imagination, and the medieval and Renaissance mind marveled with pleasure at the signs of the abundance of God.

The philosophers saw in the story of the creation a close relationship between Existence, Creation, and Goodness. The supreme lavishness of the creation reflects the supreme goodness of the Creator, for, as St. Thomas Aquinas pointed out, "Goodness and Being are really the same."[3] It is evident then that the Creator of all the diversity of earthly beings must be supremely good, for only such supreme goodness could compass the vast diversity of its creations. The mystics, too, celebrated the abundance and greatness of God:

> Almighty God, then, is named *great* in reference to His own peculiar greatness which imparts itself to all things great; and overflows, and extends itself outside of all greatness; embracing every place, surpassing every number, going through every infinitude, both in reference to its superfulness, and mighty operation, and its fontal gifts, in so far as these, being participated by all in a stream of boundless gifts are altogether undiminished, and have the same superfulness, and are not lessened by the impartations, but are even still more bubbling over. This Greatness then is infinite, and without measure and without number. And this is the pre-eminence as regards the absolute and surpassing flood of the incomprehensible greatness.[4]

Dionysius the Areopagite treats the divine attribute of abundance particularly interestingly for this study, because he uses the same symbolic

[2] The Book of Common Prayer (1549, etc.), Opening Prayer for Public Baptism, cites the justice and mercy of God in the flood. The immensity of waters is perhaps best indicated by the writer of Genesis who repeats incredulously, "the waters prevailed" (7.17-20).

[3] Thomas Aquinas, *Summa Theologica*, Pt. I, Q. v, Art. 1; Q. xliv, Art. 1, and Q. xlv, Art. 5.

[4] Dionysius, *On Divine Names*, IX, ii and iii [Parker, I, 102-103].

words that Crashaw does. "Overflows," "fontal," "stream," "bubbling over," and "flood" are typical of Crashaw's expression of divine abundance.

The concept of an abundant God Crashaw would have found on every hand.[5] This basic source idea he shaped in the manner of the typical poet of the Counter Reformation. His sensibility was by its very nature interested in the expansive and exuberant, sympathetic to the ebullient and the superfluent; and it found in the abundant generosity of the Creator and the Saviour the spiritual embodiment of a concept to which it was astonishingly akin. It could well understand this expansiveness in its divinity because it was of the same cast. Milton described the Garden of Eden as exhibiting or inducing "enormous bliss"; [6] St. Teresa prayed to her God, "Give me love abundantly." [7] Crashaw followed all his instincts in singing of the enormous bliss and abundant love of divine providence constantly outpouring for the sake of man.

It is no surprise to find the concept of abundance present in the earliest work of Crashaw, the paraphrase of the Twenty-third Psalm, written sometime before the poet was eighteen.[8] Here Crashaw has expressed the concept of abundance at least three times. For the first expression there is no source in the original: "Plenty weares me at her brest" (l. 10). The power of God is felt here essentially as protection and nourishment (see Chapter VI, Section 5), but significantly the attribute comes in large quantities; there is plenty of this protection and nourishment. The second expression paraphrases the line "Thou preparest a table before me." Crashaw writes: "Crown'd abundance spreads my Bord" (l. 50). Crashaw's interest again is in the quantity of the miraculous spread before him. His table is "Crown'd," and the word suggests at once the heaping of foods on the table and the majesty of that action. The majestic crowning is in "abundance." Crashaw again has added the concept to the original. The final expression of abundance appears a few lines later as a translation of "my cup runneth over": "How my cup orelooks her Brims!" (l. 56). The image is sharp and exciting, and it maintains the Psalmist's interest in the "superfulness" of God.[9]

[5] In the first of the Thirty-Nine Articles as well (E. Tyrell Green, *The Thirty-Nine Articles* [London, 1896], p. 25). A. O. Lovejoy traces the principle of plenitude to Plato (*The Great Chain of Being* [Cambridge, 1948], *passim*).
[6] *Paradise Lost*, V, 297; cf. *Comus*, 709-713.
[7] St. Teresa, *Poems*, II, vii ("Vuestra soy, para Vos nací . . .") [Peers, III, 280].
[8] Martin, p. xcii; the paraphrase is on pp. 102-104.
[9] This figure, peculiarly meaningful to Crashaw, reappears in the "Sospetto d'Herode" in the expression "The cup" . . . they quaffe brim full" (*ibid.*, p. 120, xlii, not in the

These three expressions of abundance all pertain to and illuminate the generosity of God in the protecting and nourishing of His flock. The Psalm prefigures the parable of the Good Shepherd (Luke 15. 3-7), and Crashaw's paraphrase stresses pastoral feeding. The royal table and the overflowing (or overlooking) cup, already remarked and, indeed, glossed in the quotation from Dionysius above, are symbols of the nourishment of God which is available and celebrated everywhere. The emphasis on the table and the cup suggests that, in keeping with a common exposition,[10] Crashaw is thinking here of the Holy Eucharist. Dionysius indicates the double nature of the abundance of the sacred food.

> Beautiful then, the super-wise and Good Wisdom is celebrated by the Oracles, as placing a mystical bowl and pouring forth its sacred drink, but first setting forth the solid meats, and with a loud voice Itself benignly soliciting those who seek It. The Divine Wisdom, then, sets forth the two-fold food; one, indeed, solid and fixed, but the other liquid and flowing forth; and in a bowl furnishes Its own providential generosities. Now the bowl, being spherical and open, let it be a symbol of the Providence over the whole, which at once expands Itself and encircles all, without beginning and without end.[11]

Crashaw evokes from the Twenty-third Psalm the allegory of the Sacrament of the Lord's Supper, a symbol of the sacrificial generosity of boundless Providence, expansive and encircling, without beginning and without end.

The same baroque interest in the abundance of this Old Testament feast animates Crashaw's treatment of the New Testament miracle of the Feeding of the Five Thousand. Crashaw has versified this miracle from John 6.1-14 eight times, regarding it, with St. John, as a type of the institution of the Lord's Supper.[12] The primary attraction to Crashaw in the retelling of this mystery is the miraculous quantity of the bread which suddenly is present. There is wonder at the ease of divine

original); in the "Apologie," "Bowles full" (p. 323, l. 33); and in the "Flaming Heart," "brim-fill'd Bowles" (p. 327, l. 99). For an examination of the baroque in Crashaw's "Psalm 23," see Imbrie Buffum, *Agrippa d'Aubigné's* Les Tragiques (New Haven, 1951), pp. 132-138.

[10] E.g., Haymo, *Sermones in Omnes Psalmos, Patrologia Latina,* CXVI, 270.
[11] Dionysius, *Letters,* IX, iii [Parker, 173-174].
[12] Martin, pp. 16, IV; 26, IV; 47, III; 56, I; 86, I; 88, III; 353, II; 399, ll. 61-64. Cf. note 53, p. 25. So clear is the Evangelist that the miracle prefigures the institution of the Last Supper that he omits that institution, dramatically described in the Synoptic Gospels.

creation from an infinitely small to an infinitely large amount. Like the
goddess, Crashaw is stupefied: "Aucta Ceres stupet arcana se crescere
messe."[13] One of the most informative treatments of the episode is
Crashaw's translation from Grotius' *Christus Patiens*:

> A subtle inundation of quicke food
> Sprang in the spending fingers, and o'reflow'd
> The peoples hunger, and when all were full
> The broken meate was much more then the whole.[14]

Crashaw develops the "inundation" from Grotius' straightforward
"creuit"; the simple increase is not enough for Crashaw, he must have
a flood. Similarly he magnifies Grotius' "Satiatus" to his own "o're-
flow'd"; his cup is not full, it is over-full; it o'relooks its brims.

From the miraculous multiplication of the loaves and fishes, three
lessons may be drawn. By the performance of the miracle, Christ teaches
the wisdom of faith in God:

> Quando erat invictæ tam sancta licentia cœnæ?
> Illa *famem* populi pascit, & illa *fidem*.[15]

By the great size of the feast (the disciples gather baskets full of the
residue[16]) Christ teaches the power of God. By the act of providing
the feast, Christ teaches the goodness of God, distributing here the
loaves and fishes as he shall soon be distributing His own flesh:

> See here an easie Feast that knowes no wound,
>   That under Hungers Teeth will needs be sound:
> A subtle Harvest of unbounded bread,
>   What would ye more? Here food it selfe is fed.[17]

The feeding of the multitude in this epigram is not merely an adequate
meal — it is a "feast," it is a "Harvest," its supply is "unbounded"; [18]

---

13 *Ibid.*, p. 16, IV.

14 *Ibid.*, p. 399, ll. 61-64, "Out of Grotius his Tragedy of Christes sufferinges."
Crashaw has translated the opening speech of the drama (spoken by Jesus). The passage
under discussion here reads: "Inter secantes dexteras creuit Ceres: / Satiatus ingens
populus, & toto tamen / Plus est relictum." George Sandys' translation, published 1640,
has: "Twixt the Dispensers Hands th' admired Bread / Increas'd, great multitudes of
People fed / Yet more than all remain'd."

15 Martin, p. 26, IV.

16 Crashaw's version, "The broken meate was much more then the whole," is certainly
more meaningful than the redactions of Grotius and Sandys. It presents a nice paradox
and suggests at the same time the virtue given to the distributed meat by contact with
Christ. The whole is not so great as the sum of its parts.

17 Martin, p. 86, I.

18 The meaning of "unbounded" can be gathered from the quotation of Dionysius:
it is an attribute of Providence which "expands Itself and encircles all, without beginning
and without end." The word occurs, for example, in the Hymn "To the Name of Iesus"

its abundance is thrice suggested. The final sentence of the epigram links the miracle with the Eucharist; in both feasts the "spending fingers" — spending themselves, that is — dispense "food it selfe."

Another instance of the concept of abundance manifested in nourishment will be found in the hymn, "O Gloriosa Domina." Crashaw sees the whole of mankind nourished by Christ as the infant Christ is nourished by His mother.

> The whole world's host would be thy guest
> And board himself at thy rich BREST.
> O boundles Hospitality!
> The FEAST of all things feeds on the.[19]

Behind the Mariolatry (and a strange mother complex which Professor Praz has pointed out[20]) is the concept of bounty. All things feed on Christ by partaking in the Eucharist of the "host," in itself not a simple dinner, but a "feast"; Christ as "host" and "guest" feeds on his mother. Mary's rich breast is thus made the general supply of the world and she the universal mother, as indeed she is named a few lines later (ll. 23-26). Here again Crashaw has introduced a reference to abundance in translating a text in which it is completely lacking.[21]

Cumulative series of images of abundance, each image more expansive than its predecessor, constitute the form of the "Song Upon the Bleeding Crucifix."[22] The structure of the poem as changed in revisions is remarkable, for not often does Crashaw seem so careful in his architectonics.[23] The poem was published first in 1646; it was structurally revised before its second publication in 1648; it received minor changes before 1652. By these revisions, Crashaw created a cruciform poem which outlined a small crucifix in the first stanza, enlarged that picture in stanzas ii-v, and concluded with a progression in the size of the

---

(Martin, pp. 239-245) where it describes that name (l. 12) and the "All-imbracing Song" of men and angels (l. 91).

[19] Martin, p. 302, ll. 7-10.

[20] Mario Praz, *Secentismo è Marinismo in Inghilterra* (Firenze, 1925), p. 152, quoted in Helen C. White, *The Metaphysical Poets* (New York, 1936), p. 203. Miss Wallerstein justly observes (*Richard Crashaw*, p. 143): "the original theme of this hymn, too, lends itself . . . to Crashaw's typical ecstasy. The resulting poem has the most of his peculiar radiance."

[21] Martin, p. 448, in a note to this poem supplies the Latin; "O gloriosa femina / excelsa supra sidera, / qui te creavit provide, / lactas sacrato ubere." The essentially Latin pun on *hospes*, "host," "guest," is not in the Latin original.

[22] *Ibid.*, pp. 288-289; earlier version, pp. 101-102. For another poem of abundance, cf. the discussion of "The Weeper" in Chap. V.

[23] *See* my "Textual Revision in Crashaw's 'Upon the Bleeding Crucifix,'" *Studies in Bibliography*, I (1948), 191-193; the alterations in the structure have been studied also by Arno Esch, *Englische Religiöse Lyric* (Tübingen, 1955), pp. 100-105.

waters. At the same time he obtained a second structural pattern, the
two acting in contrapuntal tension in the first half of the poem. The
second pattern consists of cumulative progressions in water imagery.
The first three stanzas (i-iii) shape the first series; a progression from
rivers to torrents to a flood.

> Iesu, no more! It is full tide.
> From thy head & from thy feet,
> From thy hands & from thy side
> All the purple Riuers meet.
>
> What need thy fair head bear a part
> In showres, as if thine eyes had none?
> What need They help to drown thy heart,
> That striues[24] in torrents of it's own?
>
>   Thy restlesse feet now cannot goe
> For vs & our eternall good,
> As they were euer wont. What though?
> They swimme. Alas, in their own floud.[25]

In baroque fashion, the second series expatiates on the first dramatically;[26] it begins in the fourth stanza (iv) with the simple act of giving
(not very simple here):

> Thy hands to giue, thou canst not lift;
> Yet will thy hand still giuing be.
> It giues but o, it self's the gift.
> It giues though bound; though bound 'tis free.

Though bound, the hand is capable of unbounded generosity ("free");
and it gives itself, it spends its own fingers. The drops of blood are a
rivulet of generosity.[27] The next stanza (v) moves to the abundance
of the river traditionally noted for the foison of its rich effluvium.[28]

[24] "Strives" / "striues" is the reading of the 1646 and 1652 editions; "streames" of
1648. The image is one of the heart as a swimmer struggling to keep from drowning in
a rain-swollen river.

[25] "Flood" / "floud" is the reading of 1646 and 1652; "blood" of 1648. The original
concept was "flood" as may be seen in the Latin version (Martin, p. 27) ("in fluviis
suis"), and symbolic propriety requires "flood" here.

[26] The progression is indicated by such words as these in the sequence of the stanzas:
"giues," "fruitfull . . . flowing," "payes . . . deliuer," "ouerflow," "Deliuerance." The
joint between the two series is concealed by the subject matter, the parts of the body,
and by the water imagery, which functions in both series. Hence, the poem does not
break apart between stanzas iii and iv.

[27] "It giues though bound" is the reading of 1648 and 1652; the reading of 1646 is
"It drops though bound." The deliberate revision sharpens the paradox, but it removes
the imagery of liquidity from the stanza and provides a word only superficially more
generous (see Section 2). "Thy hands to giue" is a commonplace, stemming from St.
Bernard (Rosemond Tuve, George Herbert, p. 46 n).

[28] See for example, Martin, p. 48, IV.

But o thy side, thy deep-digg'd side!
That hath a double Nilus going.
Nor euer was the pharian tide
Half so fruitfull, half so flowing.

The Nile, though doubled (perhaps to represent the water and blood),
must yield in the next stanza (vi) to a multiplicity of rivers, "innumerable" as the hairs of the head (Psalm 40.12). Even the smallest can
deliver its gift.[29]

No hair so small, but payes his riuer
To this red sea of thy blood
Their little channells can deliuer
Somthing to the Generall floud.

In stanza vii these innumerable rivers and their gifts merge in con-
fluence; the stanza following (viii) elaborates the idea.

But while I speak, whither are run
All the riuers nam'd before?
I counted wrong. There is but one;
But o that one is one all ore.[30]

Rain-swoln riuers may rise proud,
Bent all to drown & ouerflow.
But when indeed all's ouerflow'd
They themselues are drowned too.

The image of the overflowing rivers from Isaiah 8.5-8 describes the
anger of the Lord visited upon Judah for its infidelity. St. Teresa
utilizes the same image of the rain lost in the river, the river lost in
the sea to indicate the complete union which the Lord effects with His
mystical elect. In speaking of the Spiritual Marriage St. Teresa writes:

He has been pleased to unite Himself with His creature
in such a way that they have become like two who cannot
be separated from one another; even so He will not sepa-

---

[29] As Dr. Esch indicated, there is again a break here caused by the omission of the
original stanza on the thorns and roses. He argues (p. 101): "Der Verzicht auf die
Dornenkronenstrophe war im übrigen leicht, da sie keine entscheidende Bedeutung im
Aufbau besitzt. . . . Eine andere Erklärung für die Streichung, Crashaws Unzufriedenheit
mit dem 'marinistischen' Concetto der 6. Strophe, hat wenig Überzeugungskraft." The
poem remains defective, however, in terms of its cruciform structure. Dr. Esch points
out, in the first version, the relationship between stanzas 5 (head), 6 (crown), and 7
(hair). In the later version the removal of stanza 5 and the deletion of stanza 6 leaves
stanza 7 unrelated to its new predecessor (side) and with no excuse for its existence (it
should have accompanied stanza 5 to the new location or stanza 6 to limbo). In terms
of the series of progressions, this stanza has its appropriateness.

[30] "Ore" is probably a pun, though there is no parallel in Crashaw's work.

> rate Himself from her. . . . it is like rain falling from the
> heavens into a river or a spring; there is nothing but water
> there and it is impossible to divide or separate the water
> belonging to the river from that which fell from the
> heavens. Or it is as if a tiny streamlet enters the sea, from
> which it will find no way of separating itself . . .[31]

This overflowingness may be related to the love of God or to His
avenging anger. Both concepts contribute to the knowledge of His
majesty.

The general flood of these last stanzas finally acquires the dimensions
of the flood of Noah. It will be recalled that the flood was an indicator
of the Divine working in mysterious ways to proclaim the abundance
of His anger and His delivering grace. The preservation of the chosen
family and the salvation of the race through Noah, a type of Christ,[32]
redound to God's greater glory. As God showed His grace by delivering mankind from the deluge through Noah, so here (ix) through
Christ He shows His grace in a second deluge.

> This thy blood's deluge, a dire chance [33]
> Dear LORD to thee, to vs is found
> A deluge of Deliuerance;
> A deluge least we should be drown'd.

The final distich equates the abundance of these diluvial waters with
the "streams of living waters Springing from eternal love" by which all
of mankind is preserved. The bleeding upon the cross is the most
generous act conceivable to Crashaw — the greatest gift of all; such
generosity unparalleled must be described and can only be described in
terms of the greatest plenitude which Crashaw can imagine. It is thus
that the final couplet is the summation of abundance:

> N'ere wast thou in a sense so sadly true,
> The WELL of liuing WATERS, Lord, till now.[34]

---

[31] St. Teresa, *The Interior Castle*, VII, ii [Peers, II, 335].

[32] It is not demonstrable without question that Crashaw is using this typological
convention in this poem; Miss Tuve suggests the richness available to a poet (p. 73).

[33] Cf. for the same wording, Martin, p. 158, ll. 16-17.

[34] St. John of the Cross explains: "For [the beloved soul's] rejoicing is habitually so
great that, like the sea, it is not diminished by the rivers that flow from it, neither is it
increased by those that enter it; for it is within this soul that there is made that spring,
the water whereof, as Christ says through Saint John [4.5-14], springs up to eternal life"
(*Spiritual Canticle* XXIX and XXX, 8 [E. Allison Peers, *Complete Works of Saint John
of the Cross* (London, 1953), II, 143]). See also St. John 7.38 and Revelation 7.17.

Miss Mary Ellen Rickey's *Rhyme and Meaning in Richard Crashaw* (Lexington, 1961)
finds that Crashaw had a particular "rhyme vocabulary" and used certain words generally
in rhyming position to unify the poem and mark or blur the divisions. She points to

2. *Maxime in minimis*

Richard Crashaw never tired of contemplating the abundant power of God in all His works and ways. And he found cause to praise the manifestation of this power not only in its expression in infinity but in its contraction into infinitesimalness also. In noticing these divergent and paradoxical attributes of God, Crashaw was again following Dionysius. The Areopagite extended the concept of God's abundance and power around a mystical circle and observed both distribution and penetration — greatness and littleness. Of the littleness of God, he wrote:

> But *little*, i. e. fine, is affirmed respecting Him, — that which leaves behind every mass and distance, and penetrates through all, without hindrance. Yet the little is Elemental Cause of all, for nowhere will you find the idea of the little unparticipated. Thus then the little must be received as regards God as penetrating to all, and through all, without impediment; and operating, and piercing through, to "a dividing of soul and spirit, and joints and marrow"; and "discerning thoughts and intents of heart," yea rather — all things that be. For there is not a creature unmanifest in His sight. This littleness is without quality and without quantity, without restraint, without limit, without bound, comprehending all things, but itself incomprehensible.[35]

Crashaw regarded the manifestation of the little from two vantage points: he marveled first at the infinite power of God in compressing His magnitude into an infinitesimal confine and secondly at the infinite power of God in magnifying the slightest unit into immensity.

Crashaw represents this wonder in his poetry by references to small objects or units, tiny particles of the vastness of God. The simplest illustration occurs in his epigram on the parable of the widow's mites (Mark 12. 41-44):

> Two Mites, two drops, (yet all her house and land)
> Falls from a steady Heart, though trembling hand:
> The others wanton wealth foams high, and brave,
> The other cast away, she onely gave.[36]

rhyme repetitions in "Song upon the Bleeding Crucifix," in the first version as helping "to define the relationships between the four unequal sections of the lyric" (p. 28) and suggests the revisions are "in the direction of a general neatness of structure and rhyme arrangement" (p. 64). My own inclination would be to place greater emphasis on the neatness of structure.

[35] Dionysius, *On Divine Names*, IX, iii [Parker, I, 102-103].

[36] Martin, p. 86, III.

It is apparent that the widow's donation, trivial in the eyes of the world, is, in the eyes of God, one of the major financial transactions of the age. The widow's infinite generosity and God's infinite grace are resident in the cramped confines of the mites, but there is no room for them in the wanton and foaming "charity" of the wealthy.

Crashaw describes these mites as "drops," and the appositive is significant; the drop is by far the most important of the small particles in the poetry. The drop is important for several reasons. A drop serves the poet as a concrete visual image. Crashaw has deliberately and repeatedly introduced the drop into his sacred poems; the scriptural originals which he follows never specifically mention drops. A drop is interesting because of its size; it is a tiny thing capable of exerting immense power. A drop is symbolically valuable in that it is susceptible to color; it participates in the contrast of white and red (Chapter III). A drop is useful because it is liquid, and liquids of all sorts captured Crashaw's imagination (Chapter V).

Crashaw makes exact and particular the parable of Dives and Lazarus (Luke 16. 19-31) by the addition of the image of the drop.

> A Drop, one drop, how sweetly one faire drop
>   Would tremble on my pearle-tipt fingers top?
> My wealth is gone, o goe it where it will,
>   Spare this one Iewell; I'le be *Dives* still.[37]

On the tip of Lazarus' finger Crashaw has placed the drop of water and has likened it to a rich pearl. In the tiny crystal ball the baroque mystic sees all the grace of the Omnipotent, all the difference between salvation and damnation. Other rich, white drops of water are added to the account of the Baptism of Jesus in the River Jordan (Matthew 3. 13-17). Crashaw thinks of the river not generally as water but specifically as drops.

> Each blest drop, on each blest limme,
> Is washt it selfe, in washing him:
> Tis a Gemme while it stayes here,
> While it falls hence 'tis a Teare.[38]

---

[37] *Ibid.*, p. 96, I.

[38] *Ibid.*, p. 85, I. Crashaw almost versifies the scholastic dictum of St. Ambrose: "Our Lord was baptized because He wished, not to be cleansed, but to cleanse the waters, that, being purified by the flesh of Christ that knew no sin, they might have the virtue of baptism." The passage is quoted by St. Thomas Aquinas in support of his position in *Summa Theologica*, Pt. III, Q. xxxix, Art. 1. The same concept occurs in the Book of Common Prayer (1549 etc.), Opening Prayer for Public Baptism: "by the baptism of thy well beloved Son Jesus Christ, thou didst sanctify the flood Jordan, and all other waters to this mystical washing away of sin." Martin quotes in the Commentary (p. 434) a

The Baptism of Christ utilizes drops of water; the Circumcision and the Crucifixion furnish drops of blood. At the Circumcision (Luke 2. 21), Crashaw speaks of "the dear drops this day were shed"[39] and pictures each of them as equal to the whole world — "toti [gutta] par tamen unica mundo."[40] The bleeding of the infant Christ is very small, but it is in proportion to the sacrifice of the full-grown Christ on the cross. The linking of the two events was a commonplace; in one of her poems St. Teresa makes the connection between the present pain and the future passion.[41] Crashaw echoes her thought in the imagery of abundant waters:

> Tast this, and as thou lik'st this lesser flood
> Expect a Sea, my heart shall make it good.[42]

At the Crucifixion, Christ bleeds again for mankind. The crown of thorns causes drops of blood to appear on His face;[43] the nails pierce His hands to produce more blood.[44]

In writing of the blood of the Crucifixion, Crashaw is not so much interested in small drops as he is in vast quantities of blood — "Guttula quod faceret, cur facit oceanus?"[45] — representing the vast amounts of salvation and love obtained for mankind in the sacrifice; but in the discussion of this blood as represented in the wine of the Holy Eucharist, he writes again in terms of drops. Crashaw translated two of the Latin meditative hymns of St. Thomas Aquinas on the Sacrament. In one of these, "Adoro Te," this couplet occurs:

> Cuius una stilla salvum facere
> Totum mundum posset omni scelere.[46]

For the couplet, Crashaw has in his "In Adoration of the Blessed Sacrament.":

> That blood, whose least drops soueraign be
> To wash my worlds of sins from me.[47]

---

parallel from Joseph Beaumont. Cf. also St. Teresa, *Exclamations of the Soul to God,* vii [Peers, II, 407]. For the symbolic richness of the Jordan in Herbert, cf. Tuve, *George Herbert,* pp. 182-203, especially p. 184.

[39] Martin, p. 251, 1. 4.

[40] *Ibid.,* p. 53, I.

[41] St. Teresa, *Poems,* XVI, "Este Nino viene llorando" [Peers, III, 295]; and XV, "Vertiendo está sangre" [p. 294]. For additional examples of the relationship between these two events *see* Praz, *Flaming Heart,* pp. 216-217.

[42] Martin, p. 98, III. Cf. also note 97, p. 51.

[43] *Ibid.,* p. 290, I.

[44] *See* note 27, p. 18.

[45] Martin, p. 45, II.

[46] *Analecta hymnica medii aevi,* L (1907), 590.

[47] Martin, p. 293, 11. 49-50.

The change is significant. St. Thomas praises the blood because it will wash the world clean from sin; Crashaw, miserable sinner, praises it because it will wash the worlds of sin clean from Crashaw.[48] And it is the *least* drop which will have this sovereign power; the smallest particle can perform this enormous good.

The marvelous efficacy of the least drops of the sacramental wine is paralleled exactly by that of the least bits of the sacramental bread. In the free translation of Aquinas' second hymn on the sacrament, "Lauda Sion Salvatorem," Crashaw sings:

> [He,] howsoe're clad, cannot come
> Lesse then whole CHRIST in euery crumme.[49]

"Whole Christ in every crumme" is the peak of this concept of immense power in small particles. It is a beautiful line, and in it Crashaw fuses at a single stroke dogma and poetry. The image is poetically forceful, and the theology is concentrated without being impaired. It is poetry made from the doctrine of wholeness affirmed in 1551 by the Council of Trent:

> Totus enim et integer Christus sub panis specie et sub quavis ipsius speciei parte . . . exsistit.[50]

The Holy Eucharist, as noted earlier, is adumbrated by the Twenty-third Psalm and by Christ's miracle of the Feeding of the Five Thousand. Some part of the wonder Crashaw feels at these feasts derives from the way in which the miracle is performed and the table is prepared. The miracle of the Feeding (in itself a witness of God's greatness in small particles, for five loaves fed five thousand) is performed with an infinitesimal amount of effort. By merely speaking the word of

---

[48] Esch, pp. 149-150.

[49] Martin, p. 296, x, "The Hymn for the Blessed Sacrament"; the Latin original has: "Fracto demum sacramento / ne vacilles, sed memento / tantum esse sub fragmento, / quantum toto tegitur. / Nulla rei fit scissura, / signi tantum fit fractura . . ." The same idea is in Robert Southwell's "Of the Blessed Sacrament of the Aulter" [Grosart, p. 179]:
> Whole may His body be in smallest breadd,
> Whole in the whole, yea whole in every crumme;
> With which be one or be tenn thowsand fedd,
> All to ech one, to all but one doth cumme.
The concept and the rhyming *come* / *crumb* suggest that Crashaw had Southwell in mind when he wrote his lines. Southwell's poem is not a translation of "Lauda Sion," but was clearly influenced by it. Grosart observed the first stanza contained "reminiscences of Southwell's favourite hymn," (p. 181), and the present passage offers others. Southwell did translate the "Lauda Sion" as "Saint Thomas of Aquines Hymne read on Corpus Christy Daye" (pp. 144-148). The *come* / *crumb* rhyme occurs also in Herbert in a different context ("Longing").

[50] H. J. Schroeder, *Canons and Decrees of the Council of Trent* (St. Louis, Mo., 1955), pp. 73, 352; Sess. XIII, "The Holy Eucharist," chap. iii.

blessing, *eucharistos,* Christ accomplishes the miracle. It is described as "mensae faciles," "an easie Feast."[51] The "Crown'd abundance" of the table of the Twenty-third Psalm is prepared "At the whisper of thy Word."[52] The whispered Word is the voice of God, the Verbum, performing the act of creation (Psalm 33. 6, 9). But it is not a straining, loud voice (Revelation 11. 19); it is "a still, small voice" (1 Kings 19. 12). It is the same whisper that performs the marvel of the Miraculous Draught of Fishes (Luke 5. 4-11).

> Quæ secreta meant taciti tibi retia uerbi
> Queis non tam pisces, quam capis Oceanum?[53]

The secret nets catch not merely a normal draught — amazing enough on a day when the fishing has been poor — but they take what seems to be the swarm of Ocean. Similarly, the secret nets catch not merely three fishermen but three fishers of men through whom the swarm of Earth will be taken. It is all accomplished through the *tacitum verbum,* the whisper, the still, small voice.[54]

The glory of God is manifest in immense space, in tiny objects, in a whisper, and paradoxically, in a logical extension, in Nothing. God created the world from nothing, *ex nihilo;*[55] and Christ before Pilate answered Nothing (Matthew 27. 12-14). Crashaw combines into one epigram the two incidents of the power of Nothing — the creation of the world and the redemption of the world:

> O Mighty *Nothing!* unto thee,
> *Nothing,* wee owe all things that bee.
> God spake once when hee all things made,
> Hee sav'd all when hee *Nothing* said.

[51] Martin, pp. 16, IV; 86, I. Richard Hooker (*Laws of Ecclesiastical Polity* [Oxford, 1850], I. iii. 2) speaks of the intent of Moses in describing the work of creation "to signify the infinite greatness of God's power by the easiness of his accomplishing such effects, without travail, pain, or labour."

[52] Martin, p. 104, ll. 49-50.

[53] *Ibid.,* p. 358, V. The epigram is headed in Archbishop Sancroft's manuscript, the only source (Bodl. MS. Tanner 465), "Marc. 8. Pisces multiplicati." Though it can be argued that the epigram glosses the Feeding of the Five Thousand, for all his other paraphrases of this miracle Crashaw cites John 6. I should assume the Archbishop erred and that the reference is to the Heavy Draught of Fishes in John 21. 11, as Grosart suggests (II, 186), or more probably to the earlier miracle in Luke 5. 4-11 with the dramatic consequences versified in other epigrams (Martin, pp. 98, II; 358, III; 362, I). For the calling of the disciples in Matthew 4. 19, cf. p. 35, IV, and in Mark 1.16, p. 22, II.

[54] For another example *see* Martin, p. 399, ll. 65-66, referring to Matthew 8. 26: "The Wind in all his roaring brags stood still / And listned to the whisper of my will." The lines translate from the opening speech of Grotius' *Christus Patiens:* "flabra compressit notus, / Et aestuantis ira detumuit freti." Crashaw has added the "whisper."

[55] Cf. *Summa Theologica,* Pt. I, Q. xlv, Art. 2. The expression occurs at the conclusion of the section, "Respondeo . . ."

> The world was made of *Nothing* then;
> 'Tis made by *Nothyng* now againe.[56]

In the Latin original of this epigram Crashaw places the emphasis not on the Nothing from which the world was created but on the Word of creation, that is, again, the Verbum.

> *Nil ait*: o sanctæ pretiosa silentia linguæ!
> Ponderis o quanti res *nihil* illud erat!
> Ille olim, *verbum* qui *dixit,* & omnia *fecit,*
> *Verbum non dicens* omnia nunc *reficit.*[57]

When Christ confuted the Pharisees (Matthew 22. 41-46), they were not able "to answer him a word, neither durst any man from that day forth ask him any more questions."

> While they speake nothing, they proclaime
> Thee, with the shrillest Trumpe of fame.
> To hold their peace is all the waies,
> These wretches have to speake thy praise.[58]

The concept of abundant power in the Divine was one of peculiar significance to the baroque poet. Crashaw was always ready to express his wonder at God's generosity. Everywhere God manifested the effulgence of his spirit. His majesty, His mercy, His forgiveness, His self-sacrifice are all read in the overflowing life of His created nature. Even in very small objects this abundance is declared — finally, even in awe-struck silence.

3. Man's Insignificance

The plenitude of God manifests itself effectively in the immensity of His power and works. All the vastness of His outpouring nature reflects the magnificence which is His. On the other hand Man is nothing, and by his nothingness serves as a foil to suggest even more the glory of his Creator. Such doctrine abounds in Scriptural passages, and, following them in the instructions to her Foundations, St. Teresa constantly urged upon her sisters the necessity of an humble admission of their unworthiness.

> We can only learn to know ourselves and do what we
> can — namely, surrender our will and fulfil God's will

[56] Martin, p. 91, II.
[57] *Ibid.*, p. 25, II. Cf. p. 358, I.
[58] *Ibid.*, p. 92: cf. pp. 15, II; 90, I (Numbers 22. 28-30, Matthew 21. 1-7) for a humorous comment on nothing.

> in us. Anything else must be a hindrance to the soul. . .
> It causes it, not profit, but harm, for nothing but humility
> is of any use here and this is not acquired by the under-
> standing but by a clear perception of the truth, which
> comprehends in one moment what could not be attained
> over a long period by the labour of the imagination —
> namely, that we are nothing and that God is infinitely
> great.[59]

And again:

> it is absolutely true to say that we have no good thing in
> ourselves, but only misery and nothingness; and anyone
> who fails to understand this is walking in falsehood.[60]

Before the contemplation of the infinite greatness of God Crashaw was
happy to be allowed to consider his unworthy nothingness and to express
his inferiority. Other poets and preachers of the century were of the
same mind and took pleasure in pointing out the lesson to be learned
from the discrepancy between the magnitude of God and the littleness
of man. Herbert's is perhaps the best known statement:

> O rack me not to such a vast extent;
> Those distances belong to thee:
> The world's too little for thy tent,
> A grave too big for me.
>
> Wilt thou meet arms with man, that thou dost stretch
> A crumme of dust from heav'n to hell?
> Will great God measure with a wretch?
> Shall he thy stature spell? [61]

The unworthiness of man is a frequent subject in Crashaw's poems. It
may be stated directly:

> Though both my Prayres & teares combine,
> Both worthlesse are; For they are mine —[62]

and again:

> [SOVL,]
> O thou art Poore
> Of noble POWRES, I see,
> And full of nothing else but empty ME.[63]

[59] St. Teresa, *The Way of Perfection*, XXII [Peers, II, 139].
[60] *Interior Castle*, VI, x [Peers, II, 323].
[61] "The Temper," [Hutchinson, p. 55]; *see also* "Holdfast" [*ibid.*, p. 143].
[62] Martin, p. 301, xiv, "Hymn of the Church in Meditation of the Day of Judgment."
[63] *Ibid.*, p. 240, ll. 19-21, "Hymn to the Name of Jesus."

Or it may be stated in three conventional images: dust, the worm, the fly.

The origin of the significance of dust as an image for mankind is not far to seek; "the Lord God formed man of the dust of the ground" (Genesis 2.7). Throughout his life man partakes of the baseness of the lowest of the four elements. Crashaw refers to man as "Darke, dusty Man," [64] "Disdainfull dust and ashes," [65] "dry regardles dust," [66] and "son of dust," [67] and to his body as a "house of clay." [68] In these phrases Crashaw alludes anatomically to the natural state of man, theologically to the spiritual state of man. It is but fitting, as Herbert suggests, that man should be content or even appreciative of the spaciousness and welcoming brotherhood of the grave; dust he is, to dust returneth. Crashaw terms the grave or the corpse "dust" in the poems on the Gunpowder Plot and in the elegies. [69] On the Day of Judgment, when even presumptuous hills shall acknowledge their Creator and

> seek for humble Beds
> Of Dust, where in the Bashfull shades of night
> Next to their own low NOTHING they may ly, [70]

how much more then should man "couch before the dazeling light of thy dread majesty." The "Hymn of the Church on the Day of Judgment" concludes with a typical image of dust. "Dust" represents here the original substance of man to which he returns and, at the same time, it suggests the softening of his hard heart:

> O hear a suppliant heart; all crush't
> And crumbled into contrite dust.
> My hope, my fear! my Iudge, my Freind!
> Take charge of me, & of my END. [71]

The general dustiness of mankind is in sharp contrast to the sweet tears of St. Mary Magdalene [72] and to the spiritual elevation of St. Teresa. [73]

[64] *Ibid.*, p. 116, xxviii, "Sospetto d'Herode." The original has "di limo terrestre."

[65] *Ibid.*, p. 138, 1. 42.

[66] *Ibid.*, p. 238, 1. 52.

[67] *Ibid.*, p. 332, 1. 19.

[68] *Ibid.*, p. 404, 1. 34.

[69] *Ibid.*, pp. 384, ll. 29-30, and 166, ll. 11-14. The idea reappears fancifully in "The Teare," p. 85, vi.

[70] *Ibid.*, p. 245, ll. 232-235, "Hymn to the Name of Jesus." Crashaw is thinking of the predictions in Isaiah 40. 4, 64. 1-3. I take it the shades of night are blushing. *Also see* Chap. III, on the blush.

[71] Martin, p. 301, xvii. The Latin has "Cor contritum quasi cinis." "Crumbled into contrite dust" contains a bilingual pun: "contritum" means "crumbled into dust."

[72] *Ibid.*, p. 314, xxix, "The Weeper."

[73] *Ibid.*, p. 323, ll. 26-28, "An Apologie."

The flights of the latter Saint can lift man's heart; even more powerful is the love of Christ which in the wine of the Eucharist can "exalt weak EARTH" and "refine/Our dust."[74]

The most meaningful image of "dust" in Crashaw's poems occurs in the elegy on James Stanenough, Fellow of Queens' College, entitled "Death's Lecture." It is one of the two elegies originally considered secular poems which Crashaw deemed worthy to be included in the final *Carmen Deo Nostro*. The poet imagines himself standing beside the grave looking in on the corpse. The handful of dust which he sees before him is the goal and purpose of life, is the final end of life, is life itself, is the frailty of man, is the Platonic idea of man. All man's worthless nothing lies in the close and cold bed. Crashaw invites man to look into the grave as into a mirror to see virtue her own feature, scorn her own image, and the very age and body of the man his form and pressure.

> Come man;
> Hyperbolized NOTHING! know thy span;
> Take thine own measure here: down, down, & bow
> Before thy self in thine idæa; thou
> Huge emptynes! contract thy self; & shrinke
> All thy Wild circle to a Point. O sink
> Lower & lower yet; till thy leane size
> Call heaun to look on thee with narrow eyes.
> Lesser & lesser yet; till thou begin
> To show a face, fitt to confesse thy Kin,
> Thy neighbourhood to NOTHING. . . .
> This posture is the braue one this that lyes
> Thus low, stands vp (me thinkes,) thus & defies
> The world. All-daring dust & ashes! only you
> Of all interpreters read Nature True.[75]

To "read Nature True" is to recognize man's utter and complete nihility, to practice the humility of St. Teresa.

There is another image of dust that Crashaw uses occasionally. It is one of clouds of dust blown by the wind, but Crashaw equates this dust too with mortality. St. Teresa uses the image; in the *Interior Castle* dust is metaphorically the cares of "possessions or honours or business."[76] The dust particles blow into man's eyes and prevent his contemplating

---

[74] *Ibid.*, ll. 44-45.

[75] *Ibid.*, pp. 340-341, ll. 10-32. Cf note 65, p. 44.

[76] St. Teresa, *Interior Castle*, I, ii [Peers, II, 210-211]; *see also ibid.*, VI, iv [Peers, II, 290]; *Life*, XX [Peers, I, 129]; *Way of Perfection*, XIX [Peers, II, 81] *Conceptions of the Love of God*, VII [Peers, II, 398]; *Thoughts and Maxims* [Peers, III, 269].

the love of God. They are exhalations of man's own nature or making, and they blind him. Herbert has the same thought in "Love" (II):

> Our eies shall see thee, which before saw dust;
> Dust blown by wit, till that they both were blind.[77]

The image appears with particular relevance in "The Epiphanie Hymn":

> No longer shall the immodest lust
> Of Adulterous GODLES dust
> Fly in the face of heau'n.[78]

The poet is thinking specifically of Persian and Egyptian religions as they are superseded by Christianity. The dust is thus naturally associated with the sandstorms of the desert. The evil deeds of men — the motes in the eyes of the pagans — will no longer (1) disturb the sight of heaven by blinding it, nor (2) defiantly and perversely oppose the divine will.

The second image which Crashaw uses consistently for the nothingness of man is the worm. The figure is readily explained by the baseness of the animal which like the serpent, crawls always on its belly. Again there is Biblical authority: Job 25.4-6, Ps. 22.6. Donne and Herbert both construe man as a worm, and St. Teresa utilizes the image very often to indicate the miserableness of man and the "unsavory" quality of this earthly life.[79] "We, low Wormes,"[80] Crashaw calls mankind, and he speaks of the pagan sun worshipers as "All-Idolizing wormes."[81]

A third image that suggests man's worthlessness, his foolishness, his evanescence, and his obsession with depravity is the fly. The fly is traditionally the image for frivolity and wantonness; man is "a silly flie," according to Herbert.[82] Crashaw describes this world as containing:

> painted shapes,
> Peacocks & Apes,
> Illustrious flyes,
> Guilded dunghills, glorious L Y E s.[83]

[77] [Hutchinson, p. 54].

[78] Martin, pp. 256-257, ll. 102-104; see also Chap. IV. "Lust" and "dust," a rhyming pair Crashaw liked to use, occurs also in Herbert (in the sonnet cited in note 77.)

[79] St. Teresa, Interior Castle, I, i; VI, iv [Peers, II. 202, 290].

[80] Martin, p. 242, l. 109.

[81] Ibid., p. 257, l. 114. See also 280, ll. 9-10.

[82] "Complaining" [Hutchinson p. 143]; Herbert refers to "summer friends" as flies in "The Answer" [ibid., p. 169 and n., p. 536].

[83] Martin, p. 332, ll. 11-14, "To the Same Party Counsel."

He uses the image specifically also to refer to courtiers:

> those gay flyes,
> Guilded ith' Beames of earthly kings;
> Slippery soules in smiling eyes.[84]

It is interesting to observe the connection in Crashaw's mind between flies and slipperiness. Here the courtiers are "Slippery soules" basking in the influence that streams from an earthly king's "smiling eyes." The attributes reek of the uncertainties of political intrigue in an atmosphere such as that described above. A courtier again, or possibly merely a gallant, is described as a "slippery Pair / Of false, perhaps as fair, / Flattering but forswearing eyes" and the god of him and of others like him is the "god of flyes," presumably Beelzebub.[85]

"Charitas Nimia" expresses the "abasement of man," as Miss Wallerstein has put it,[86] by the three images that have been mentioned in this section.[87] The poet is astonished, as he so often is, by the magnitude of the love which will allow the Son to give himself for the sins of man. The fact is never mentioned, but the tone of incredulity which permeates the poem is one of the most forceful elements in its success. The contrast between the magnificence of the Creator and the miserableness of the creature is repeated constantly. The poem begins with the question that has troubled poets and philosophers since the Psalmist worded it: "Lord, what is man?" Crashaw echoes Psalm 144. 3-4, Prayer Book version specifically, but the same question appears in Psalm 8. 4 and Job 7. 17.

> Lord, what is man? why should he coste thee
> So dear? what had his ruin lost thee?
> Lord what is man? that thou hast ouerbought
> So much a thing of nought?   (1-4)

Crashaw elaborates the concept with his concrete images. The image of dust suggests the storms of mortality.

> Let froward Dust then doe it's kind;
> And giue it self for sport to the proud wind.
> Why should a peice of peeuish clay plead shares
> In the Æternity of thy old cares?   (29-32)

---

[84] *Ibid.*, p. 250, ll. 91-93, "The Nativity Hymn." Despite this attitude, Crashaw sued for the assistance of Queen Henrietta Maria in 1646.

[85] *Ibid.*, p. 329, ll. 57-59, 51; *see also* p. 338, l. 7. There are Scriptural analogues. "Beelzebub" means in Hebrew "god of the flies"; he is also "the chief of the devils" (Luke 11.14).

[86] Ruth Wallerstein, *Richard Crashaw*, p. 54.

[87] Martin, pp. 280-282. *See also* Chap. VI, Sec. 7.

The worm represents the baseness of man, groveling on this little earth.

> Should not the king still keepe his throne
> Because some desperate Fool's vndone?
> Or will the world's Illustrious eyes
> Weep for euery worm that dyes;   (35-38)

The fly is man's frippery and frivolity:

> Will the gallant sun
> E're the lesse glorious run?
> Will he hang down his golden head
> Or e're the sooner seek his western bed,
> Because some foolish fly
> Growes wanton, & will dy?   (39-44)

III. WHITE AND RED

WHITE AND RED are for Crashaw the primary colors of poetry. Mr.
Warren has observed that one cannot survey Crashaw's imagery "without perceiving how the whole forms a vaguely defined but persistently
felt series of interrelations. There are things red—fire, blood, rubies,
roses, wine— and things white— tears, lilies, pearls, diamonds: symbols
of love and passion; symbols of contrition, purity, innocence."[1] There
are indeed two groups of things opposed in color and opposed in symbolic values; their member images recur with almost tedious frequency
in the poetry. This chapter will examine these images and symbols and
clarify their interrelations, vaguely felt and persistently defined, by a
judicious rearranging and supplementing of Mr. Warren's list of things
white and red. So there are flowers—lilies and roses—and there are
gems—pearls or diamonds and rubies— and there are liquids—tears or
water and blood or wine. After an excursus into sources, the following pages will notice first the flowers and then the gems. The most
conspicuous set of color images is that involving the liquids; as it is extensive and as it has its own integrity, it appears separately in Chapter
V. There are other white substances and liquids—snow, silver, milk,
cream, crystal—but they do not regularly stand in color opposition and
they may conveniently be noticed in the poems as they occur; there is
fire, which is red only occasionally and which does not stand in color
opposition.[2] There is, however, one other thing white and red—the
blush; it neatly and appropriately combines the two colors. Finally
there are many adjectives of color which Crashaw uses to expand the
pattern. In line after line, he joins substantives and attributives in a
manner which demonstrates unmistakably that he is thinking in terms
of the white and red contrast and of its symbolic values.

To speak of sources for the white/red color distinction is perhaps to
mislead; it is more nearly accurate to trace traditions or to cite suggestions. The white/red contrast was very much in the air when Cra-

---

[1] Austin Warren, *Richard Crashaw*, p. 192.
[2] The primary symbolic values of fire in Crashaw are heat and light, communicating
the love of God (Chap. VI, Sec. 2). The iconography of the Church represents fire
as red, with particular reference to Pentecost, but Crashaw seems generally to have
resisted this tradition.

shaw began to write. It occurs, occasionally, for example, in Southwell, and with regularity in the poems of d'Aubigné; it is a marked characteristic of many of the painters of the baroque.[3] The result of Crashaw's interest in these colors — the poet was also a painter — is a pattern which is peculiarly Crashavian, which Crashaw uses with consummate skill to considerable effect, and of which the reader must be aware to understand the nuances of the poetry.

The first suggestion for the contrast and the one which reflects the most important theological significance comes from Isaiah and the Passion and underlies many images in the sacred poetry of the Renaissance. The Prophet refers to the remission of the red sins of man by the cleansing power of the whiteness of divinity: "Come now and let us reason together, saith the Lord: though your sins be as scarlet, they shall be white as snow; though they be red like crimson, they shall be as wool."[4] Donne follows the tradition:

> Oh make thy selfe with holy mourning blacke,
> And red with blushing, as thou art with sinne;
> Or wash thee in Christs blood, which hath this might
> That being red, it dyes red soules to white.[5]

So does Herbert:

> Thy bloudy death and undeserv'd, makes thee
> Pure red and white,[6]

and Vaughan writes:

> [Christ's] pure blood did flow
> To make stain'd man more white then snow.[7]

The second suggestive source for the contrast is the colors of the bread and wine of the Eucharist. This source does not yield the wealth of connotation that the former does, but in some passages the poet is evidently thinking of the color distinctions of the creatures of the Mass. The third suggestive source is the natural color of the dawn or Homer's observation of that color (unless Nature and Homer are the same). The pink pastels of the dawn's light, recalling the lushness of Rubens,

---

[3] Buffum, *Agrippa d'Aubigné's Les Tragiques*, pp. 76-83; E. I. Watkin, *The English Way* (London, 1933), p. 288, quoting Praz.

[4] Isaiah 1.18. To the Hebrews wool was the color of snow (Psalm 147.16; Revelation 1.14). *See also* Psalm 51.7.

[5] Donne, "Holy Sonnets," iv, 11-14 [Grierson, I, 323].

[6] Herbert, "Dulnesse" [Hutchinson, p. 115]; *see also* Tuve, *George Herbert*, pp. 149-151.

[7] Vaughan, "Ascension-Hymn" [Martin, p. 483]; *see also* "As Time One Day" [p. 512].

form one of the family of reds. The fourth suggestive source is the Petrarchan tradition of amorous poetry.[8] The color contrast appears as a commonplace in sixteenth- and seventeenth-century secular lyrics, and it weaves a meaningful strand in *Venus and Adonis*.[9]

The color distinction pervades a rich and highly involuted complex of symbols, and its powers of suggestion and connotation are among the most extensive in Crashaw. White represents purity and the effect of cleansing. The purest soul or person shares the divine purity of absolute white, but there are off-whites to suggest the innocence of others. Whites perhaps most frequently color tears. Tears are white because they are the evidence of repentance and contrition; they symbolize the first step that the sinner must take up the ladder of perfection to the blessedness of pure white. Red is basically the blood of the sacrificed Lamb, and it symbolizes the great love of God and His Son as revealed in the Passion. Through the image of the blush, however, red stands also for the fleshly shame and the sinfulness of man. Hence the typical Christian paradox: the red blood (divine love) can wash white as snow the red sins of man (mortal shame). The love of God comes to man as the dawn comes, and Crashaw has a ramified set of images to suggest this manifestation. The contrast between these two colors figures in almost every poem; any interpretation of Crashaw must consider it.

The first of the symbolic contrasts predicated on the distinction between white and red is composed of flowers: lilies and roses. It is well to recall the Biblical references to these flowers. The first occurs in Isaiah (35.1) in a passage foretelling the birth of the Messiah.[10] The Vulgate and the King James versions provide differing translations:

> et exsultabit solitudo, et florebit quasi lilium;
> and the desert shall rejoice, and blossom as the rose.[11]

A second well-known mention of the lily, in Matthew 6.28-29, describes its native and undecorated beauty and compares it favorably to Solomon in all his glory: "Considerate lilia agri quomodo crescunt . . .

---

[8] *See* for example Crashaw's own secular verse: "Wishes. To his (supposed) Mistresse," Martin, p. 196, ll. 31-54, and "Out of the Italian. A Song," p. 188. The original of this song, written in 1596 by Ansaldo Cebà, contains the same color contrast. Perhaps this tradition stems from Song of Songs 5.10.

[9] Hereward T. Price, "Function of Imagery in *Venus and Adonis*," *Papers of the Michigan Academy of Science, Arts, and Letters*, XXXI (1945), 287, 288, 293-295.

[10] So considered by St. Thomas Aquinas, for example (*Summa*, Pt. III, Q. xxxv, Art. 6).

[11] The Vulgate "lilium" is an inexact rendering of the Hebrew *chabatstseleth*; the only other occurrence of the word in the Bible is at Song of Solomon 2.1, where the Vulgate again inexactly translates "flos campi." This translation may, however, have suggested Crashaw's "Candide rex campi" in the epigram quoted below. For some of the particular symbolic associations of these flowers, *see* Henry Hawkins, *Parthenia Sacra* (Aldington, Kent, 1950), pp. 17-37.

Dico autem vobis, quoniam nec Salomon in omni gloria sua coopertus est sicut unum ex istis." This expression of the simplicity and beauty of the lily Crashaw paraphrased in one of his epigrams.

> Candide rex campi, cui floris eburnea pompa est,
>> Deque nivis fragili vellere longa toga;
> Purpureus Solomon impar tibi dicitur. esto.
>> Nempe (quod est melius) par fuit ille rosis.[12]

Crashaw's comment on the passage characteristically contributes the rose to complete the color pattern. Solomon is said to have been unlike the lily; he must consequently have been like the rose. And how much more fitting this is! The whiteness of the lily implies its complete purity, its nearness to God; the redness of the rose associates it with the color of carnality. Solomon, purple in his raiment and his flesh, is but a mortal sinner. The third reference to roses and lilies is familiar in the King James version (Song of Solomon 2.1): "I am the rose of Sharon, and the lily of the valleys." Herbert and Vaughan both were moved by this verse — the former declared the presence of God in His created world (and rejected secular love poetry):

> *Roses* and *Lillies* speak thee; and to make
> A pair of Cheeks of them, is thy abuse;[13]

and the latter addressed Christ Himself:

> O rose of *Sharon*! O the Lilly
>> Of the valley!
> How art thou now, thy flock to keep,
> Become both *food*, and *Shepheard* to thy sheep.[14]

Jesus is referred to as a lily in order to represent poetically His purity and His unadorned beauty. The drops of blood shed at the Circumcision transform this unstained whiteness into unstained redness (divine love) or stained redness (mortal sin):

> Ah ferus, ah culter! qui tam bona lilia primus
> In tam crudeles jussit abire rosas.[15]

The lily Christ comes into this world and begins almost immediately to be tainted with the redness of man's sins; He is ". . . this modest maiden lily / Our sins haue sham'd into a rose."[16] The purity of the

---

[12] Martin, p. 354, III.
[13] Herbert, "Sure, Lord, there is enough" [Hutchinson, p. 206].
[14] Vaughan, "Holy Communion" [Martin, p. 458].
[15] Martin, *Crashaw*, p. 365, III, ll. 1-2.
[16] *Ibid.*, p. 251, ll. 11-12, "New Year's Day." This is 'gilding the lily.' The image reappears at p. 256, ll. 82-83. The color is red or gold.

Infant Christ illuminates the Infant Martyrs who died in consequence of Herod's proclamation (Matthew 2.16). As Herod was searching for Christ, it is only just that the Innocents who were slaughtered in His place should receive their reward. Crashaw liked the story of the infant martyrdom and treated it several times.[17] Twice he compared the mothers' milk and the infants' blood to lilies and roses.

> To see both blended in one flood
> The Mothers Milke, the Childrens blood,
> Makes me doubt if Heaven will gather,
> *Roses* hence, or *Lillies* rather.[18]

The red rose decks the birthplace of the Infant Christ, and Crashaw implies that the Babe emits the beauty of the flower.

> Cernis ut illa suo passim domus ardeat auro?
> Cernis ut effusis rideat illa rosis?
> Sive aurum non est, nec quae rosa rideat illic;
> Ex oculis facile est esse probare tuis.[19]

And in a grim paradox at the death of Christ, the crown of thorns causes drops of blood (roses) to bloom on Christ's head.[20]

The second of the symbolic contrasts is formed of gems: pearls or diamonds and rubies. A gem has its own individual worth, but it often combines with others to form a diadem. This action raises the gems to a power of circular perfection, a crown of glory. The rhyme assists.

White gems in general partake of either the purity of heavenly virtue or the contrition of mortals. The water of baptism with which John baptized Christ was imaged as a gem and a tear. The little white drop of water on the tip of Lazarus' finger was a pearl containing quantities of heavenly Grace. Pearls and diamonds are the images most closely and frequently associated with tears, the sign of an humble and a contrite heart. The image of the tear as a pearl is a commonplace in Renaissance poetry. Shakespeare writes:

> The liquid drops of tears that you have shed
> Shall come again, transformed to orient pearls.[21]

---

[17] He may have been indebted to Southwell, "St. Peter's Complaint," xciv [Grosart, p. 34]: "Sweet roses, mixt with lilies, strow'd your hearce, / Death virgin-white in martyrs' red did steepe; / Your downy heads, with pearles and rubies crownd . . ." The slaughter is the theme also of Marino's *La Strage de gli Innocenti*, and Prudentius uses some of the same color imagery in *Cathemerinon*, xii, "Hymnus Epiphaniae," ll. 111-128.

[18] Martin, p. 95, II; Latin version, p. 37, III.

[19] *Ibid.*, p. 51, III.

[20] *Ibid.*, p. 290, I. Cf. note 72, p. 117.

[21] *Richard III*, IV. iv. 321-322. *See also Parthenia Sacra*, pp. 189-198.

The small teardrop, "the liquid jewell of a teare," [22] possesses much more value than would be expected of so small an object. Tears are "Sorrowes best Iewels" [23] and the best decoration that contrition can assume. The tears of the Magdalene are the most distinctive tears in the canon; they are often described as pearls. Teardrops, as another sort of pearl, represent the dew of morning or evening.

> Such a Pearle as this is
> (Slipt from *Aurora's* dewy Brest)
> The Rose buds sweet lip kisses.[24]

> The purest Pearles, that wept her Evening Death.[25]

In these lines the pearls replace the dewdrops for ornamental effect. The meaning is straightforward and figurative without being complex, though, as the dew was thought to be heaven-sent, these pearls might contribute the whiteness of divine grace. The diamond is an alternative to the pearl.

> What bright soft thing is this?
> Sweet *Mary* thy fair Eyes expence?
> A moist sparke it is,
> A watry Diamond; from whence
> The very Terme, I think, was found
> The water of a *Diamond*.[26]

Or the diamond may stand for the eye, with a cluster of connotations. The Madonna and Child look at one another:

> Shee 'gainst those Mother-Diamonds tryes
> The points of her young Eagles Eyes.[27]

One more white "gem" of great value concludes the list, ivory, though the image is rare. Christ is described as "Virgineüm hoc . . . ebur," and the color reflects His purity.[28] In an epigram already cited, the adjective colors the "pomp" of the lily ("Candide rex campi, cui floris eburnea pompa est").

---

[22] Martin, p. 401, l. 24.

[23] *Ibid.*, p. 80, viii, "The Weeper," 1646 version; omitted in later versions.

[24] *Ibid.*, p. 84, iv, "The Teare."

[25] *Ibid.*, p. 168, l. 19, "Upon the Death of Mr. *Herrys*."

[26] *Ibid.*, p. 84, i, "The Teare." "Water" was, and is, the term for the transparency and luster of the diamond. Crashaw also defines natural phenomena by the symbolic in "The Weeper" (p. 309, iv).

[27] *Ibid.*, p. 108, xii, "A Hymn of the Nativity"; omitted in final version. "Tryes The points" is a process of testing or sharpening; "Eagles Eyes" recalls the bestiary tradition (cf. *Batman vppon Bartholome* [London, 1582], f. 176ᵛ). For the eagle, *see* Chap VI, Sec. 1.

[28] Martin, p. 365, III, l. 3.

Of red gems Crashaw distinguishes only the ruby. The drops of
red blood shed at the Circumcision are compared to the bright red
coloring of the morning.

> Bid thy golden GOD, the Sun, . . .
> Put all his red-ey'd Rubies on;
> These Rubies shall putt out their eyes.[29]

Christ's blood is brighter and more beautiful than the red streams in
the firmament; it represents strikingly His love for mankind.

The contrast between white and red gems occurs frequently. Though
no specific gem is mentioned, Dives' purple clothing, bejeweled, so to
speak, with ruby flames in Hell, presents the difference effectively.

> Rich *Lazurus*! richer in those Gems, thy Teares,
> Then *Dives* in the Roabes he weares:
> He scornes them now, but o they'l sute full well
> With th'Purple he must weare in Hell.[30]

The white tears of poor Lazurus typify greater wealth than the purple
clothing of opulent Dives. The white drop on Lazurus' pearl-tipped
finger and the white drops of his tears both represent divine favor.

The epigram "On the wounds of our crucified Lord," juxtaposing
the blood of Christ's feet nailed on the cross and the tears of Mary
Magdalene, incorporates the imagery of white and red flowers and
gems.[31] Seeing Mary at the Crucifixion (Mark 15. 40), Crashaw recalls the earlier episode (Luke 7. 36-50) when she had kissed Christ's
feet and washed them with her tears.[32] The feet of the crucified Christ
must pay back these kisses and tears through the wounds made by the
nail. Hence (stanza ii) the wounds must be both mouth and eye.[33]

> Lo! a mouth, whose full-bloom'd lips
> At too deare a rate are roses.
> Lo! a blood-shot eye! that weepes
> And many a cruell teare discloses.

[29] *Ibid.*, p. 251, ll. 13-16, "New Year's Day."

[30] *Ibid.*, p. 89, II. There may be a pun intended on "sute" in the third line. Dives'
purple robes and flames must have been an extremely popular emblem and device, for
Falstaff has apparently seen a representation in "the painted cloth" (*1 Henry IV*,
III. iii. 36; IV. ii. 27).

[31] Martin, p. 99. The Latin original provides the name of the Weeper (p. 41, IV).
See also pp. 44-45, 87, 98-104.

[32] Warren, p. 134. Herbert has a poem on the same subject, "Marie Magdalene"
[Hutchinson, p. 173].

[33] The medical word for the borders of a wound is, and was in 1640, *lips; Richard III*,
I. ii. 56: "Dead Henry's wounds / Open their congeal'd mouths and bleed afresh."
Wounds are imaged as eyes again in another epigram, Martin, p. 43, I.

The first two lines are red — "mouth," "bloom'd," "lips," "roses"; the second two are white — "eye," "tear." But the eye, being bloodshot, is itself a concentrated image of the white/red contrast. Stanza iv:

> This foot hath got a Mouth and lippes,
>   To pay the sweet summe of thy kisses:
> To pay thy Teares, an Eye that weeps
>   In stead of Teares such Gems as this is.

The purpose of these paradoxes is now apparent. The Magdalene's kisses from her lips and tears from her eyes are both to be repaid (v),

> The difference onely this appeares
>   (Nor can the change offend)
> The debt is paid in *Ruby*-Teares,
>   Which thou in Pearles did'st lend.

In the third line of this stanza the red blood and the white tears condense into the phrase, "*Ruby*-Teares"; the red gems which are drops of blood from the mouth-wound assimilate with the white gems which are tears from the eye-wound. In a commercial image, Christ pays the debt of tears in blood; He satisfies the obligation, though He makes the payment in currency of another color (*See* Chapter VI, Section 7). Unfortunately, at this point Crashaw deserts the logic of the structure which has been promising a fair apportionment to both tears and kisses, and, in the sudden condensation, he forgets the kisses. Crashaw assures us that Mary "shal . . . have all repaid,/Whatsoe're [her] charges were," but he fails to repay the kisses in the contract.

The blush is another of the Crashavian substantives which depend on the relationship of red and white. The image is common in Renaissance poetry, and Shakespeare employs it with full cognizance of its red and white contrasts.

> The roses fearfully on thorns did stand,
> One blushing shame, the other white despair.[34]

It occurs as well in Spenser:

> The ioyous day gan early to appeare,
> And faire *Aurora* from the deawy bed
> Of aged *Tithone* gan her selfe to reare,
> With rosie cheekes, for shame as blushing red.[35]

[34] Sonnet 99. *See also Love's Labour's Lost,* I. ii. 96-113, for more on the white and red and the blush.
[35] *Faerie Queene,* I, XI. li.

Crashaw uses the blush in two distinct senses. One blush is the blush of modesty. This coloring flushes the cheeks of maidens and those of unquestioned purity. The second blush is the blush of shame — "the burnish of . . . sin" [36] — and results from the attempt to conceal a sin. Miss Wallerstein has pointed out the progression in the development of the image from the juvenilia of an ingenious schoolboy to the final poems with their rich symbolic significances, but she has not indicated this distinction. [37] The simplest use of the term is for the purpose of showing a red color; a field of battle red with the blood of soldiers is a "blushing ground." [38] Generally, the image describes the cheek of an individual or a personification. Cheeks begin as white as snow, and they may become "nests of new roses." [39]

The blush of modesty is applied to infants and to those of pure character. Brides — as traditionally — blush modestly. [40] Mary's modesty reveals itself in a blush which, though red, does not stain her purity. It contrasts, however, with the white light of the moon (another chaste goddess) and the stars.

> Whose blush the moon beauteously marres
> And staines the timerous light of starres. [41]

And the little lips of the infant Christ blush the pure red of the rosebud: "the red leaves of thy Lips, / That in their Buds yet blushing lye." [42] A particular example of the blush of modesty has been much commended. It occurs in the epigram on the Water Changed to Wine, as the first miracle that Christ wrought in Cana of Galilee (John 2. 1-11).

> Unde rubor vestris, & non sua purpura lymphis?
> Quæ rosa mirantes tam nova mutat aquas?
> Numen (convivæ) præsens agnoscite Numen:
> Nympha pudica Deum vidit, & erubuit. [43]

---

[36] Martin, p. 197, l. 65.

[37] Ruth Wallerstein, *Richard Crashaw*, pp. 132-134.

[38] Martin, p. 158, l. 17.

[39] *Ibid.*, p. 343, l. 39.

[40] *Ibid.*, p. 343, l. 28.

[41] *Ibid.*, p. 302, ll. 3-4, "O Gloriosa Domina." Crashaw's syntax is not perfectly clear in the passage; "blush" can be the subject or object of the verbs. It is probably the subject; Mary, herself free of stain, cannot mar or stain except beauteously. Much concerned with Mary's modesty, Crashaw wrote one English and two Latin epigrams on it (*ibid.*, pp. 27, II; 89ₓ, I; 354, V) (*see* note 84, p. 100). The Virgin is called the Moon in "A Hymn to St. Teresa" (p. 320, l. 123). For Mary's blush *see Parthenia Sacra*, pp. 19-20.

[42] Martin, p. 108, xii, "A Hymn of the Nativity"; omitted in final version. The action described is presumably nursing. Praz, *Flaming Heart*, pp. 248-249.

[43] Martin, p. 38, IV. The commentary on the epigram is large: Martin, pp. 429-430, xcii-xciii; Praz, pp. 211-213.

The quatrain has been translated many times, but no translator has captured the beauty of the original nor done so well as Crashaw himself in animating Grotius' account:

> Drinke fayling there where I a guest did shine
> The Water blush'd, and started into Wine.[44]

The blush of shame is applied to those who have something to hide or who recognize that they are guilty of sin. It is in this explication of the blush that the major symbolic significance exists.

> With blushing Cheek & bleeding ey,
> The conscious colors of my sin
> Are red without and pale within.[45]

Crashaw expresses the conflict in the colors of white and red three times in these lines: the white cheek has blushed to red, the white tears of the eye are bleeding red, and the heart, conscious of its guilt, is ashen white in contrition, sending its red blood into the cheeks.

Less spectacularly — almost playfully, one might say — the image colors St. Teresa's youthful voyage to the Moors and martyrdom. Crashaw commends the child but notes practically,

> Scarse has she Blood enough to make
> A guilty sword blush for her sake.[46]

The conscious colors of man's sins are white and red, and they show that they are by appearing in flushed cheeks. It is only the whiteness of the broken body and the redness of the Redeemer's blood in the Eucharist which together can wash the scarlet sins of man and make him white as snow (Psalm 51.7).

Whiteness has several tints and several attributive adjectives. Uncomplicated or pure *white* symbolizes primarily divine purity and is closely associated with the "light" of the next chapter which is basically the Good. Pure white pertains most frequently to the Godhead. Crashaw uses the adjective for Christ himself [47] and in a spirit of devout

[44] Martin, p. 399, ll. 51-52, "Out of Grotius." The original lacks the lines.

[45] *Ibid.*, p. 301, xi, "Hymn of the Church in Meditation of the Day of Judgment." The original has "Culpa rubet vultus meus." Cf. Southwell, "Mary Magdalen's Blushe," l. 1 [Grosart, p. 59].

[46] Martin, p. 317, ll. 25-26, "Hymn to St. Teresa." There is another image of the blush in this poem (ll. 153-154): "[St. Teresa's] wounds shall blush to such bright scarres / As keep account of the LAMB's warres." This appears to be a reference to the Saint's stigmatization, but as far as I can tell, she was never so honored (V. Sackville-West, *The Eagle and the Dove* [London, 1943], p. 53); the "Lamb's warres" must refer to the transverberation.

[47] Martin, p. 282, ll. 57-58; p. 294, iii. St. Teresa speaks of the whiteness of her Lord's hand (*Life*, XXVIII [Peers, I, 183]).

humility aspires no higher than to Christ's feet. The final destination of mankind is the Lord's white feet. Crashaw advises that man "crowd for kisses from the LAMB's white feet"; [48] that mankind walk with Christ "whereso'ere he setts his white/ Stepps." [49] The Virgin Mary is St. Teresa's "white/ MISTRESSE." [50] The raiment and feathers of angels are white.[51] The Resurrection of Christ is recorded in "joyes white Annals." [52] *Snowy* is another shade of whiteness. The dove which represents the Holy Ghost has a snowy back; [53] the company of heaven surrounding the Virgin is her "snowy family;" [54] the pure maiden's bosom is a "snowy fortresse of defence." [55] Another adjective of white is *silver*. In devotional and secular poems it describes a mountain stream,[56] the tears of Cupid,[57] and the hairs of old age.[58] But its important symbolic use in Crashaw is in the expression of the purity of mortals and saints. It shares with white gems the connotations of value. In the "Ode" prefixed to a prayer book, Mrs. M. R. is termed a "silver breasted dove." [59] The Virgin is also described as silver: "the dear immortall doue / Sighes to his syluer mate." [60] *Milky* is yet another adjective of whiteness. In the religious poetry it refers often to the Milky Way in a punning pattern found, for example, in the next paragraph. But it can represent mortal penitence or purity. The eyes of the Magdalene are "nests of milky doues" [61] in "The Weeper"; hence it is hardly surprising in the same poem to find also cream, the most excellent and desirable part of milk.

A more important variant of white is *crystal*. Like silver it is at once a color of purity and a substance of value. It partakes of the purity of whiteness in that it is the substance from which are made the Heavens

[48] Martin, p. 261, 1. 14.
[49] *Ibid.*, p. 321, ll. 179-180.
[50] *Ibid.*, p. 320, ll. 123-124; cf. p. 306, l. 63.
[51] *Ibid.*, p. 130, l. 11. Cf. 57, I, for a contest in whiteness between Mary and the annunciation angel. In keeping with Church tradition which regarded Mary as superior even to the angels, here she is described as whiter than the white angel.
[52] *Ibid.*, p. 100, l. 10.
[53] *Ibid.*, p. 243, l. 159.
[54] *Ibid.*, p. 320, l. 127.
[55] *Ibid.*, p. 328, l. 17. The gentlewoman described has also a "white bosom" (l. 16), and another young lady has a "white hand" (p. 131, l. 18, "On Mr. G. Herberts booke.").
[56] *Ibid.*, p. 94, l. 8; p. 103, l. 15.
[57] *Ibid.*, p. 160, l. 61.
[58] *Ibid.*, p. 168, l. 31.
[59] *Ibid.*, p. 129, l. 92; the adjective is omitted in the final version.
[60] *Ibid.*, p. 304, ll. 7-8.
[61] *Ibid.*, p. 311, xv. It is hard to say exactly what Crashaw means by these doves (tears). They possess by virtue of their whiteness some heavenly purity, but they share no other qualities of the dove as symbol (Chap. VI, Sec. 1.) Christ's eyes are doves in Southwell, "St. Peter's Complaint," lxxiii [Grosart, p. 29].

(Revelation 21.11) and the concentric spheres. Spenser describes the sphere of Heaven in "The Hymne of Heavenly Beautie":

> And last, that mightie shining christall wall,
> Wherewith he hath encompassed this All.[62]

Crashaw's cosmos too is built of this substance; heaven is "the Christall globe," [63] and the harmonious spheres are crystalline. In the "Hymn in the Glorious Assumption," the Virgin mounts "through the crystall orbes, clearer then they / . . . and makes a farre more milkey way." [64] On earth by an extension of the image, a pure soul in a pure body may be "sheath'd in a christall shrine." [65] Only the building material of heaven is pure enough for the mortal flesh of the pure and temperate Christian. The waters of the River Jordan like those of the River of Life (Revelation 22.1) are melted crystal.[66] *Pearly* shares with crystal connotations of purity and value. It occurs rarely, though the noun is frequently met.

"The Weeper" contains all of these shades of white.[67] There are touches of red which flash occasionally also, but the poem is essentially a study and impressionistic painting in whites. It is as well an extraordinary example of the concept of liquidity, but this aspect of the poem belongs in Chapter V. The white characteristics of Mary's tears are symbolic of the fact that, as she has been purified by her contact with Jesus, her weeping is the evidence of her contrition. Her tears witness to divine mercy, showing mankind the importance of repentance. The symbols of whiteness begin with the opening lines: the eyes of the Magdalene are "Parents of syluer-footed rills! [the Lamb is white-footed] / . . . Thawing crystall! snowy hills" (i). Her tears are the cream that "floates aboue" the "milky riuers" of heaven (iv). Paralleling the redness of the morning, here "the euening's eyes / . . . Red with weeping are" — a white/red concentration (vi). The Magdalene's tears are Sorrow's "proudest pearles" (vii). The white dew prefers serving as the Saint's tears to adorning two white flowers: "The primrose's pale cheek" and "the lilly's neck" (viii). The "watry Blossom" of the Saint's eyes — her white tears — when ripe (*i. e.*, red) "will make the richer wine": white tears bloom to red wine (xi). The

---

[62] "Hymne of Heavenly Beautie," ll. 36-47. Cf. note 82, p. 99.

[63] Martin, p. 384, l. 23. With this spelling it is difficult not to believe a pun is intended.

[64] *Ibid.*, p. 304, ll. 5-6. The Milky Way is the traditional pilgrimage way to heaven. For Crashaw's universe *see* Chap. VI, Sec. 8.

[65] *Ibid.*, p. 343, l. 23; the same idea expressed Platonically, p. 195, ll. 10-12.

[66] *Ibid.*, p. 112, xi.

[67] *Ibid.*, pp. 307-314; earlier version on pp. 79-83.

same color contrast occurs in the next stanza; angels fill their "crystall violls" (cf. Revelation, *passim*) with "Their master's Water: their own Wine" (xii).

Stanza xiv implies a color combination based on the image of the blush. The cheeks of the Magdalene in which the "faithfull flowres" of May lie smiling — she is blushing — agree with her eyes from which the "kinder showres" are falling (xiv). The white April showers bring (red) May flowers; the Saint has "Fountain & Garden in one face" (xv). This white and red concentration reveals the subtlety of the image. The repentance of the Magdalene has earned the forgiveness of Christ:

> The lamb hath dipp't his white foot here.   (xviii)

The Saint is a mint; she coins "syluer shoures" (xxi); then she spends — "Still spending, neuer spent" (i) — her wealth prodigally, "Euen to the last Pearle" in her treasury (xxii).[68]

The poem concludes with two stanzas in which the tears respond to the poet's direct questions. In the first one the tears will not become dew again for two red and blushing (?) flowers (having previously left two white flowers in stanza viii): "The rose's modest Cheek / Nor the violet's humble head" (xxx). Nor will they become "gemmes" or even "Diadems." They go, as in the epigram "On the wounds of our crucified Lord," to meet

> A worthy object, our Lord's FEET.   (xxxi)

"Mary in the New Testament is always found at the feet of our Lord."[69]

The ramifications of white are matched by shades of red; *red, purple, ruby,* and *rosy* are the principal colors, but *ruddy, crimson,* and *vermillion* occur also. *Red* is the basic color. Examples of this adjective are too numerous and obvious to require explication; one will suffice: "Every red letter / A wound of thine"[70] now spells salvation for man. *Purple* is a shade of red which adds the concept of royalty to the divine love, or, by transference, it may heighten the sense of sinfulness. It may refer simply to the grape, the vine, and the blood of humans; it

---

[68] The color silver is linked with the gold of the Saint's hair; the two precious metals constitute riches greater than those of princes (xx). It is hardly surprising to find also that the Weeper's silver is more valuable than gold, in the opinion even of the river renowned for its golden sand (xiii).

[69] J. N. Davies, "Mark," *Abingdon Bible Commentary* (Nashville, 1929), p. 1016.

[70] Martin, pp. 86-87, ll. 6-8, "On the still surviving markes of our Saviours wounds." Cf. my "Richard Crashaw and the Little Gidding Bookbinders," *N & Q*, CCI (January 1956), 9-10. *See also* note 80, p. 118.

may signify the royal blood of Christ in the Circumcision; [71] and with connotations of the magnificence of the sacrifice, it may figure the Crucifixion itself.

> Larg throne of loue! Royally spred
> With purple of too Rich a red.[72]

The consummate image suggests the red blood of Christ's death, the royalty of the death and its magnificence, and the redness of man's sin for which only the absolute whiteness of Christ can atone:

> Why should the white
> Lamb's bosom write
> The purple name
> Of my sin's shame? [73]

The color *ruby* refers on its simplest level to a bright red sunrise. Crashaw speaks of "the Ruby portalls of the East." [74] It conveys connotations of great wealth also, as in the epigram "On the wounds of our Crucified Lord." The contrast with white is natural, but Crashaw might have found it in Lamentations 4.7.

One admirable passage includes all these reds and introduces the fourth one, *rosy*. In the "Hymn to the Name of Jesus," Crashaw discusses the persecution by the Roman gladiators of the Christian martyrs, Christ's "old Friends of Fire" whose blood is "That impatient Fire":

> What did their Weapons but sett wide the Doores
> For Thee: Fair, purple Doores, of loue's deuising;
> The Ruby windowes which inrich't the EAST
> Of Thy so oft repeated Rising.
> Each wound of Theirs was Thy new Morning;
> And reinthron'd thee in thy Rosy Nest,
> With blush of thine own Blood the day adorning.[75]

The passage is a brilliant succession of reds. The wounds of the martyrs made by the swords of the gladiators are first "purple Doores" suggesting the royalty of the martyrs' deaths, then "Ruby windowes" suggesting the richness and the value of their deaths, and then the "Rosy nest"

---

[71] Martin, p. 310, xi; p. 30, I; p. 385, ll. 63-64; p. 365, III, ll. 3, 4; two more shades of purple are given in the Latin: "ab ostro" and "muricis."

[72] *Ibid.*, p. 278, v, "Vexilla Regis."

[73] *Ibid.*, p. 282, ll. 57-60, "Charitas Nimia." Cf. note 80, p. 118.

[74] *Ibid.*, p. 113, xvi. Praz, p. 235. It is interesting to observe how often Crashaw couples this adjective with windows or casements. *See* Chap. VI, Sec. 4.

[75] Martin, p. 245, ll. 198, 214, 216-222. For study of this hymn, *see* Louis L. Martz' *The Poetry of Meditation* (New Haven, 1954), pp. 331-352. For comment on the fire and the nest *see* Chap. VI, Secs. 2, 5.

of Christ, suggesting the protection and salvation secured through His blood which has ignited the blood of the martyrs with the red fire of love. But most striking in the conceits is the idea, clear throughout, that the wounds of the martyrs testify to the dawn of a new day, the day of the true light (a red / white contrast). This dawn / day concept is suggested through the images of doors and windows, magic casements opening to something new, and through the adjective traditional for the dawn, "rosy." Crashaw has given the ancient Homeric color rich Christian significance. This "rosy MARTYRDOME" [76] leads in the dawning of the new day of Christ.

Though Crashaw uses the adjective *rosy* also to describe wine, Saints, angels, and the Virgin, [77] he thinks regularly of the inescapable link between rosy and the dawn and feels in each use of the word infant beatings of some great promise to be fulfilled. This close association predicates a concept of things becoming, a dynamic nascent symbol. [78] As the dawn leads in the day, so the promise is fulfilled, the earnest expectation is manifested, hope is satisfied and defined, [79] types yield to truths, and Law submits to Grace. Christ, *cuius nomen est Oriens,* is the dawn, the day-spring (*Vulgate*: "Oriens") from on high who "hath visited us, To give light to them that sit in darkness and in the shadow of death, to guide our feet into the way of peace" (Luke 1. 78-79). The Incarnation is

> The day-break of the nations; their first ray
> When the Dark WORLD dawn'd into Christian DAY. [80]

So the Virgin's "healthfull womb" was "the Rosy DAWN that sprung the Day." [81] The old law yields to the new truth when it "spyes loue's dawn." [82] The poet appeals to the Messiah: "O dawn, at last, long look't for Day!" [83]

The image of the dawn suggests the East; and the richness of the East, seen specifically in the magnificence and opulence of the Kings in the "Epiphany Hymn," is summed up in the image of Arabia, a land vastly wealthy in spices and redolent of rare perfumes: "exceeding rich

[76] Martin, p. 337, l. 48.

[77] *Ibid.,* p. 323, l. 43; p. 321, l. 172; pp. 325, l. 32, and 326, l. 67; p. 306, l. 60.

[78] Buffum rightly observes that one characteristic of the baroque style is the emphasis "on becoming rather than being; . . . Crashaw has certainly done everything possible to heighten the impression of evolution and movement" (*Agrippa d'Aubigné's* Les Tragiques, p. 134).

[79] Martin, p. 345, l. 4.

[80] *Ibid.,* p. 261, ll. 3-4, "To the Queen's Majesty."

[81] *Ibid.,* p. 303, ll. 18, 21, "O Gloriosa Domina."

[82] *Ibid.,* p. 295, iv.

[83] *Ibid.,* p. 243, l. 149, "Hymn to the Name of Jesus."

in all those things which we esteem most precious." [84] Crashaw sings a "Hymn to the Name of Jesus":

> SWEET NAME, in Thy each Syllable
> A Thousand Blest ARABIAS Dwell;
> A Thousand Hills of Frankincense;
> Mountains of myrrh, & Beds of spices,
> And ten Thousand PARADISES.[85]

The reference to Paradise, to the Garden in Eden, accounts for some part of the value of Arabia, but Arabia was traditionally always a place of riches and astonishing creatures; not the least remarkable of the latter was the 'rare Arabian bird," the phoenix.

> Bring hither all the BLEST
> ARABIA, for thy Royall Phœnix' nest.[86]

The symbolic significances of this bird are manifold (Chapter VI, Section 1). Some part of the richness of the East lies in its spices and perfumes. The nest of the phoenix (another nascent symbol) is made of cinnamon and frankincense, and when the image is transplanted to a Christian society and literature, the scent comes too. Religion is instructed to bring with it "whatsoe're perfum'd thy *Eastern nest.*" [87] The tomb of Christ is called "faire Immortalities perfumed Nest." [88] As He rises, Christ is enveloped in a mandorla of perfuming exhalations "Dropping with a baulmy Showr / A delicious dew of spices." [89] But the most luscious of the images of scent and perfume is the long passage in "The Hymn to the Name of Jesus" (ll. 165-182).

> O thou compacted
> Body of Blessings: spirit of Soules extracted!
> O dissipate thy spicy Powres
> (Cloud of condensed sweets) & break vpon vs

---

[84] Diodorus, *Bibliotheca Historica*, III, 45, quoted in Allan H. Gilbert, *A Geographical Dictionary of Milton* (New Haven, 1919), "Arabia," p. 27. For the location of Eden in Arabia, *see A Dictionary of the Bible*, ed. James Hastings (New York, 1911), "Eden."

[85] Martin, p. 244, ll. 183-187.

[86] *Ibid.*, p. 275, Hymn, "Office of the Holy Cross." The Latin text is "Conditur aromate, complentur scripturæ" [Maskell, *Monumenta Ritualia Ecclesiae Anglicanae*, III, xii]. Only in John does the expression "the scripture should be fulfilled" occur here, and it does not refer to the embalming. The embalming at the time of the entombment occurs also in John, and the action is performed by Nicodemus. Crashaw has conflated the events and introduced the figure of his beloved Magdalene (specifically from Matthew 28.8). One of the activities of the community at Little Gidding was the preparation of Gospel harmonies; such preparation would have led to such conflation.

[87] Martin, p. 138, l. 10. For further comment on the nest, *see* Chap. VI, Sec. 5.

[88] *Ibid.*, p. 100, II. "Perfumed" literally, by Nicodemus (John 19. 39-40) and figuratively, because it is "eastern."

[89] *Ibid.*, p. 331, ll. 109-110.

In balmy showrs;
O fill our senses, And take from vs
All force of so Prophane a Fallacy
To think ought sweet but that which smells of Thee.
. . . In none but Thee
And Thy Nectareall Fragrancy,
Hourly there meetes
An vniuersall SYNOD of All sweets;
By whom it is defined Thus
That no Perfume
For euer shall presume
To passe for Odoriferous,
But such alone whose sacred Pedigree
Can proue it Self some kin (sweet name) to Thee.

Other rich associations with the dawn are suggested by the two meanings of "spring," vernal season and water source, both senses of the word connoting the nascent symbol. The latter sense employs the synonyms "fount" and "fountain." The fertile season betokens the abundant harvest which is to follow; the water source develops into a stream of great size.

Water'd by the showres they bring,
The thornes that thy blest browes encloses
(A cruell and a costly spring)
Conceive proud hopes of proving Roses.[90]

The crown of thorns planted on Christ's head, produces drops of blood which are roses. The thornes bring showers, the showers of April; and the image is primarily one of the spring season. But as the stanza appears in the early version of one of Crashaw's most "liquid" poems, the idea of the stream is appropriate also. The drops of blood become a river. A clear instance of the image of the water source is the vision of Christ's eyes as "The blissfull springs of joy"[91] from which sun and stars drink their luminosity. Spring, the season, "All the yeare doth sit and sing,"[92] a characteristic which is reminiscent of Christ's "so oft repeated Rising," each martyr's death being a new morning of the revelation of love. Another example recalls the color contrast which is behind the symbolic interpretation of the dawn and the spring. Jesus

---

[90] *Ibid.*, p. 101, ll. 21-24, "On the bleeding wounds of our crucified Lord"; omitted in final version. *See also* note 29, p. 19. For the spring-harvest relationship, Martin, p. 349, ll. 33-37 (in final version only), and p. 96, IV (the appropriate couplet is omitted in later versions).

[91] *Ibid.*, p. 267, Hymn.

[92] *Ibid.*, p. 102, l. 6. *See also* note 73, p. 72; note 24, p. 88.

is "The rich & roseall spring of those rare sweets." [93] The word "spring" is intentionally an ambivalent nascent symbol. Jesus is the spring because he is the source of all sweet things and because he is the climate that promises the harvest. He is the rich spring, because he promises them continuously and abundantly. He is the roseal spring because he has shed his red blood for mankind and because like the dawn he foretells the wonder, beauty, and fulfillment of the new, rich day.

Yet another facet of the nascent symbol exists in the image of the bud of the rose. It is readily seen that the blowing bud is at once the sign of spring and the cognate of the dawn.

> And, through the *Night* of error and dark doubt,
> Discerne the *Dawne* of Truth's eternall ray,
> As when the rosie *Morne* budds into Day.[94]

At Christ's birth the "babe's bright face" is "the purpling Bud / And Rosy dawn of the right Royall blood." [95] As the bud image is applicable at the birth of Christ, which is the beginning of His earthly ministry, so is it at the Resurrection, which is the beginning of His heavenly intercession for man. The tomb of Joseph of Arimathea is the rock which "buds forth the fountaine of the streames of Day." [96] In the same way that Moses' rod brought water from the rock and rescued the Israelites thirsting in the wilderness (Numbers 20.11), here from the rock which has entombed Him, Christ in two nascent images rises as a fountain of light or unfolds as a white, perfumed bud. He is also a stream of light and love to the thirsting world which can be satisfied only through his sacrifice.

The Feast of the Circumcision of Christ is celebrated on the first of January. By virtue of this date the Feast Day is a nascent or beginning time. Furthermore, the blood of the Circumcision by its color suggests the red dawn, or beginning, imagery. In addition, the little drops of blood, in themselves evidencing the abundance of God, prefigure the greater shedding of blood at the Crucifixion and, therefore, like the dawn or the rosebud, herald greater things to come. The concept of growing informs the structure of one of Crashaw's epigrams on the

---

[93] *Ibid.,* p. 331, 1. 116.

[94] *Ibid.,* p. 191, ll. 12-14, "On the Frontispiece of *Isaacson's* Chronologie."

[95] *Ibid.,* p. 261, ll. 5-6, "To the Queen's Maiesty." Grosart (I, 93) is disturbed by this image; I cannot agree that "purpling Bud" refers to the three Kings.

[96] Martin, p. 100, II, 1. 9, "Easter day." This image recurs in the Latin epigram p. 353, IV. Miss Tuve points out in Herbert and in the tradition the relationship between the striking of Moses' rock and the striking of Christ's side (*George Herbert,* pp. 27-28, 68); the idea is transferred in Crashaw (if it exists).

Circumcision: from death to life, youth to maturity, hope to realization, dawn to day, weeping to dying, buds to tree, knife to spear.

> To thee these first fruits of my growing death
> (For what else is my life?) lo I bequeath. . . .
> Now's but the Nonage of my paines, my feares
> Are yet but in their hopes, not come to yeares.
> The day of my darke woes is yet but morne,
> My teares but tender and my death new-borne.
> Yet may these unfledg'd griefes give fate some guesse,
> These Cradle-torments have their towardnesse.
> These purple buds of blooming death may bee,
> Erst the full stature of a fatall tree.
> And till my riper woes to age are come,
> This knife may be the speares *Praeludium.*[97]

The splendid image of the bud of the purple rose, which is figured in the drops of blood shed by the Infant, growing to a full-blooming and full-bleeding tree, the cross, is one of Crashaw's more effective epigrammatic conceits. The thoroughness of the growth image, it should be noted, is developed after the publication of the Latin original of the poem, which has no lines that can pass for a source for most of it. This development is an example of the maturing of Crashaw's imagery and symbolism.

"In the Holy Nativity of our Lord God A Hymn Sung as by the Shepheards" utilizes the color of rose and the imagery of the dawn with the particular liturgical purpose of celebrating the Feast of the Nativity;[98] its closely related companion piece, "In the Glorious Epiphanie of our Lord God, A Hymn. Sung as by the Three Kings," celebrates the Feast of the Epiphany.[99] Mr. Warren notes that the relationship of the two hymns invites speculation.[100] It does, indeed, and one aspect of that relationship is the imagery of color which reflects their historical

---

[97] Martin, pp. 98-99, ll. 1-2, 9-18, "Our Lord in his Circumcision to his Father." The Latin original is p. 38. I. Cf. also pp. 251-252, "New Year's Day."

[98] *Ibid.*, pp. 246-251. For earlier version see pp. 106-108. Any study of this poem must be. much indebted to Kerby Neill, "Structure and Symbol in Crashaw's *Hymn on the Nativity*," *PMLA*, LXIII (March 1948), 101-113. I have not seen it noted that the "source" for this hymn is an eight-line epigram of Crashaw's, written presumably in the 1630's. It is entitled "In natales Domini Pastoribus nuntiatos" (Martin, p. 355, IV). One of the shepherds in it is named Tityrus, and it closes with the shepherd / lamb conceit.

[99] Martin, pp. 253-361; cf. also pp. 69-70.

[100] *Richard Crashaw*, p. 151. Some of their relationship becomes evident in the positions they occupy in the printed editions. In 1646 the Nativity Hymn is unrelated to "A Hymn for the Circumcision day." In 1648 these two hymns together with the newly written Epiphany Hymn stand contiguously in proper order of the church year. In 1652 they repeat this order but it is a part of the liturgical order of the life of Christ; this arrangement is presumably the care of Car.

and theological backgrounds. The two poems express two states. In
the "Nativity Hymn" Christ's birth is sung by the Hebrew shepherds
to whom He has been shown in His first manifestation (the day spring
from on high hath visited us): it is the dawn, the promise of a new
beginning. Christ is the glory of His people Israel. In the "Epiphany
Hymn" Christ's epiphany is sung by the Gentile Kings to whom He
has been shown in His second manifestation (to give light to them that
sit in darkness): it is the day, the fulfillment of a new life to the Gentiles. Christ is a light to lighten the Gentiles (Luke 2.32). The two
states are figured in the imagery: the "Nativity Hymn" is rich in imagery
of the dawn and the Orient — white and red; the "Epiphany Hymn"
is rich in imagery of the day — white and black.

St. Luke recounts that after worshiping the Christ child "the shepherds returned, glorifying and praising God for all the things that they
had heard and seen" (2.20) and that "they made known abroad the
saying which was told them concerning this child" (2.17). Crashaw
supposes the shepherds returning from their tremendous midnight en-
lightenment and awakening the morning sun to sing their dawn song
to him.

> Come we shepheards whose blest Sight
> Hath mett loue's Noon in Nature's night; [101]
>   Come lift we vp our loftyer Song
> And wake the Svn that lyes too long.
>   (1-4)
>
> Tell Him He rises now, too late
> To show vs ought worth looking at.
>   (9-10)

In its rise, the supernatural sun has superseded the natural, a theme
which is to be more fully developed in the "Epiphany Hymn," a hymn
of the noonday sun. Forgetting the sun now, the two shepherds sing
alternate verses describing the effects of the Babe's eyes. Tityrus sings
that even in the night these eyes emanated light; the new day of
Christianity

> was THY day, SWEET! & did rise
> Not from the EAST, but from thine EYES.
>   (21-22)

The day that rises is a new kind of dawn; Christ is his own East. Like
Venus, Aurora must go shift.[102] The promises of this new dawn will be

---

[101] Cf. for the same light images, Herbert, "Christmas" and "The shepherds sing"
[Hutchinson, pp. 80-81].
[102] Martin, p. 13, ll. 83-86: "cede improba mater."

kept. Thyrsis, the second shepherd, extends the metaphor; the eyes are not only the dawn, they are also the spring. So in the dead of winter

> The North forgott his feirce Intent;
>   And left perfumes in stead of scarres. . . .
> Where he mean't frost, he scatter'd flowrs.
>   (26-29)

The flowers of spring — though no color is specified — are probably red to contrast with the white of the frost and to recall that the stable has elsewhere been decked with roses.[103] "The Weeper" has already described the flowers of May as red, and these same flowers bloom at the end of this poem. The flowers of spring bring their own perfumes, and "perfume" is one of the words associated with the imagery of the East.

The two shepherds combine to sing the glory of yet another nascent image, Mary.

> We saw thee in thy baulmy Nest
>   Young dawn of our æternall DAY!
> We saw thine eyes break from their EASTE
>   And chase the trembling shades away.
>   (31-34)

Mary's womb has already been noted as the rosy dawn; she is herself here the "Nest" — a symbol of becoming — from which the fledgling will fly to His own tree. The nest is "baulmy" for several reasons: it is surrounded by the fragrant perfumes of the benignant North Wind; it exudes its own sweet savor of the Orient; [104] it drops balm, a healing restorative and an attribute suitable to the Virgin; and specifically it is made of spicy and aromatic twigs, for it is the nest of the phoenix.

> The Phænix builds the Phænix' nest.
>   Love's architecture is his own.
>   (46-47)

The Incarnation and the Resurrection compress into this single, striking image, "symbol at its purest and richest, concentrated and clarified . . . by the now mature integration of the imagination of its maker." [105]

---

[103] *Ibid.*, p. 51, III.

[104] The womb is traditionally a "nest of spicery"; cf. *Richard III*, IV. iv. 424.

[105] Wallerstein, p. 132. The image considerably improves Southwell's comparable use in "The Nativity of Christe," ll. 1-2 [Grosart, p. 128]: "Behould the father is His daughter's sonne, / The bird that built the nest is hatchd therein."

"He that made all things, had not done," Crashaw writes, "Till he had made Himself thy son." [106]

> The BABE whose birth embraues this morn,[107]
> Made his own bed e're he was born.
>
> (48-49)

The next section of the poem contrasts neatly the colors of white and red, reconciling their differences in the Child and His Mother. Christ has built His own nest, but Nature wishes to supply Him with gifts. The snow offers itself as sheets, but its offer is rejected:

> Your fleece is white But t'is too cold.
>
> (56)

The whitest natural object on earth though perfectly white is too cold. It possesses perhaps something of the quality of sterility. It is too pure; it is not sufficiently vital.[108] At the other extreme is the gift of "the obsequious SERAPHIMS" who wish to bestow "Their rosy fleece of fire." [109] Once again the offer is rejected:

> are you sure
> Your down so warm, will passe for pure?
>
> (62-63)

The reddest natural object in heaven though perfectly red is too hot. It possesses perhaps something of passionate carnality. Its color is impure; it is not sufficiently divine.[110] What will serve? Nothing but the Virgin.

> See see, how soon his new-bloom'd CHEEK [111]
> Twixt's mother's brests is gone to bed.
> Sweet choise, said we! no way but so
> Not to ly cold, yet sleep in snow.
>
> (67-70)

[106] Martin, p. 302, ll. 5-6, "O Gloriosa Domina." Cf. p. 35, I, and p. 23, III (less appositely). Tuve, p. 142 n.

[107] For a gloss on "embrave" see Martin, p. 252, l. 21, "New Year's Day."

[108] Mr. Neill suggests that "perhaps it is too material to be moved by love" (p. 106).

[109] The color here was originally purple, not rosy. The "source" epigram has "Purpureus juvenis gaudia tanta vehit." Crashaw changed the "officious Angels" in the version of 1646 to "obsequious SERAPHIMS" in the version of 1648 and gained thereby the reference to fire and to rose. The seraph who visits St. Teresa is "Rosy" (Martin, p. 325, ll. 27-28, 31-32; Chap. VI, Sec. 2). Dionysius describes the fire of the Seraphim in *The Celestial Hierarchy*, XV, 2. (Cf. Neill, p. 107.) For a gloss on "obsequious," *see* Martin, p. 118, xxxiii.

[110] The alleged impurity of the angels is difficult to understand. Mr. Neill presents a recondite source for the idea which Crashaw quite possibly knew, but it seems to me the taint of the color is the nearer way.

[111] The adjective "new-bloom'd" is an addition to the 1652 version.

The Christ lays His red cheek between the white breasts of His Mother. She alone has all the cool, white purity and all the warm, red love required for

> Æternity shutt in a span.
> Sommer in Winter. Day in Night.
> Heauen in earth, & GOD in MAN.
>
> (80-82)

She alone has the gift of divine abundance in her maternity. Her breasts are full of cool, pure, white milk; [112] her lips give warm, pure, red kisses. Hence:

> WELCOME. Though nor to gold nor silk.
> To more then Cæsar's birthright is; [113]
> Two sister-seas of Virgin Milk,
> With many a rarely-temper'd kisse
> That breathes at once both MAID & MOTHER,
> Warmes in the one, cooles in the other. [114]
>
> (85-90)

The shepherds conclude their Hymn of welcome with a reminder of the spring:

> Yet when young April's husband showrs
> Shall blesse the fruitfull Maja's bed
> We'l bring the First-born of her flowrs
> To kisse thy FEET & crown thy HEAD.
>
> (97-100)

The shepherds' crown will be one of flowers — not of thorns — which will kiss with their red lips the Lamb's white feet. The following passage recalls the reader deftly to the shepherds and their flocks and brings him back to the fields of Palestine on Christmas morning.

> To thee, dread lamb! whose loue must keep
> The shepheards, more then they the sheep. . . . [115]
> Each of vs his lamb will bring
> Each his pair of syluer Doues;

[112] Cf. Martin, p. 302, ll. 7-10, "O Gloriosa Domina."

[113] Two views of Caesar's birthright are given in Martin, pp. 54, IV; 96, II. For the richness of the concept in Herbert's "The Sacrifice," see Tuve, pp. 27-30.

[114] There followed in the versions of 1646 and 1648 a stanza rich in color: "Shee sings thy Teares asleepe, and dips / Her Kisses in thy weeping Eye, / Shee spreads the red leaves of thy Lips, / That in their Buds yet blushing lye . . ." (Martin, p. 108, xii). Though it adds much to the symbolic color scheme of the poem, it disrupts the structure of the 1652 version more, and its omission is a gain in unity (Neill, p. 111). See also Praz, pp. 248-249.

[115] The "source" epigram poses valuable questions in this context: "Ipse Deus cum Pastor erit, quis non erit agnus? / Quis non pastor erit, cum Deus Agnus erit?"

Till burnt at last in fire of Thy fair eyes,
Our selues become our own best SACRIFICE.
(101-109)

The final quatrain suggests the fulfillment of the New Covenant, re-placing the old tradition of animal sacrifice with the revealed experience of human and personal sacrifice; [116] and the last couplet, through its paraphrase of the Prayer of Consecration in the Holy Eucharist, includes all sinners, inviting them to participate in the Oblation, to reject the silver doves and to burn in the red fire of Christ's eyes. The fire is the fire of divine love [117] which illuminates those eyes symbolically with the light of the dawn of the Christian Day and with the warmth of the spring of the New Year.

[116] *See further* Crashaw's epigram, "Christus infans Patri sistitur in templo," Martin, p. 54, I, and ll. 43-48 in "On a Treatise of Charity," pp. 138-139. The rhymed pair recurs.
[117] *See* Martz, pp. 165-166, and Chap. VI, Sec. 2.

IV. LIGHT AND DARK

THE SOURCE of the second color contrast in Crashaw is the Bible. God manifests the distinction between light and dark, like the concept of abundance, in the opening verses of Genesis. The Judaeo-Christian tradition will trace its emphasis on this opposition back to these verses, though the idea is fundamental and exists in pre-Hebraic and pagan cultures.[1] Dionysius the Areopagite, devotes several ecstatic chapters of the *Divine Names* to the description of of the actions and characteristics of God as Light. As a commentary on the symbolism of light in Crashaw his remarks are valuable.

> Let us then now celebrate the spiritual Name of Light, on the ground that He that fills every supercelestial mind with spiritual light, and expels all ignorance and error from all souls in which they may be, and imparts to them all sacred light, and cleanses their mental vision from the mist which envelops them, from ignorance, and stirs up and unfolds those enclosed by the great weight of darkness, and imparts, at first, a measured radiance; then, whilst they taste, as it were, the light, and desire it more, more fully gives Itself, and more abundantly enlightens them, because "they have loved much," and ever elevates them to things in advance, as befits the analogy of each for aspiration.

> The Good then above every light is called spiritual Light, as fontal ray, and stream of light welling over, shining upon every mind, above, around, and in the world, from its fulness, and renewing their whole mental powers, and embracing them all by its over-shadowing; and being above all by its exaltations; and in one word, by embracing and having previously and preeminently the whole sovereignty of the light-dispensing faculty, as being source of light and above all light, and by comprehending in itself

[1] Warren, *Richard Crashaw*, p. 178. *See also* Harry Levin, *The Power of Blackness* (New York, 1958), pp. 29-31, and Francis B. Gummere, "On the Symbolic Use of the Colors Black and White in Germanic Tradition," *Haverford College Studies*, I, (1889), 112-162.

all things intellectual, and all things rational, and making them one altogether.[2]

Dionysius stresses the equation that the Good is Light. He indicates also the abundant quality of this outpouring Light. His concepts that Light originates in God and that it is the source of the intellect and the inspiration of rational activity harmonize with Crashaw's exposition of the symbol. Ultimate truth is revealed to the mystic in the love and illumination of the divine Light. St. Teresa similarly described the Divine Light in her visions of the Divine Presence.

> It did farre exceed all that, which can possibly be imagined in this world, by the verie clearnes, and brightnes thereof. Nor yet is it anie such brightnes, as dazles; but a brightnes, which is accompanied, with a most sweet kind of beautie; a brightness, I say, there is infused, which giues extreame delight to the sight, and which is farre from wearying it; nor doth the light thereof, also offend, whereby we see this object of so Diuine Beautie. This, I say, is a light, so very different from all that, of this inferiour world, that euen the brightnes of the Sunne it self, which we see, is so dimme, and dull a thing, in comparison of that claritie, and light, which is represented to our sight by this meanes, that euen the eyes would scarce open themselues, to behold it. For it is, as if it were a most pure water, running all vpon Christall, with the Sunne reflecting vpon it, and striking through it; in comparison of some other, which were of a muddie kind, and in a clowdie day; and which were running also vpon earth. Not yet, that there is anie Sunne represented in it; nor is that Light like the Light of the Sunne; for, in fine, this Light of the Vision, seemes a very naturall Light; whereas the other is but a kind of artificiall thing, in comparison thereof. This is a Light, which neuer sets; but as it is euer Light, so is there nothing, which can disturbe it; but in fine, it is a thing of such a kind, as that, how sublime soeuer the vnderstanding of anie Creature might be, he would neuer, in all the dayes of his life, be able to conceiue rightly, what kind of thing it were.[3]

This description of light expresses as well as can be done in terms other than those of light itself, the light of the love of God incandescent in the mystic, glowing like the filament within the bulb.

---

[2] Dionysius, *Divine Names*, IV, v and vi [Parker, I, 38-39].
[3] St. Teresa, *Life*, XXVIII [*Flaming Hart* (1642), pp. 390-391]. *See also Conceptions of the Love of God*, IV [Peers, II, 384].

The connection between the sun of the solar system and the celestial light is at once apparent. St. Teresa relates the natural sun to the celestial radiance. The sun is the feeble and inadequate embodiment of the light of heaven. It serves as a symbol Platonically for celestial illumination and may be regarded as a hieroglyph of the divine. In this very pertinent page of the *liber creaturarum* may be read the magnificence and the abundant, life-giving love of God. The importance of the sun as symbol appears in Dionysius.

> But, what would any one say of the very ray of the sun? For the light is from the Good, and an image of the Goodness, wherefore also the Good is celebrated under the name of light; as in a portrait the original is manifested. For, as the goodness of the Deity, beyond all, permeates from the highest and most honoured substances even to the lowest; so, too, the brilliant likeness of the Divine Goodness, this our great sun, wholly bright and ever luminous, as a most distant echo of the Good, both enlightens whatever is capable of participating in it, and possesses the light in the highest degree of purity, unfolding to the visible universe, above and beneath, the splendours of its own rays, and if anything does not participate in them this is not owing to the inertness or deficiency of its distribution of light, but is owing to the inaptitude for light-reception of the things which do not unfold themselves for the participation of light.[4]

The goodness of Light in the persons of the divine, the love of the divine towards man, the Platonic representation of the divine idea in the actuality of the sun: these are the primary levels on which the symbol of light may be said to have connotative value. Other specific correlations exist in the change between Judaism and Christianity; the Light became flesh and dwelt among us.

The force opposing the goodness of Light is the evil of dark. As God is the zenith of Good and Light so is Satan the nadir of Evil and Darkness. "The way of the wicked is as darkness," Solomon observed. "But the path of the just is as the shining light, that shineth more and more unto the perfect day" (Proverbs 4.19, 18). Crashaw's attitude to darkness parallels St. Teresa's. To him as to her, sin is dark, and the sinning soul lives "In utter darkness . . . far removed from God and light of Heavn."

[4] Dionysius, *On Divine Names*, IV, iv [Parker, I, 36-37].

> I want you to consider what will be the state . . . when
> the soul falls into a mortal sin. No thicker darkness exists,
> and there is nothing dark and black which is not much
> less so than this . . . since the soul has separated itself from
> Him, it cannot be pleasing in His eyes; for, after all, the
> intention of a person who commits a mortal sin is not to
> please Him but to give pleasure to the devil; and, as the
> devil is darkness itself, the poor soul becomes darkness it-
> self likewise.[5]

There is no need further to labor the contrast of light and dark.
Crashaw takes the symbolic images as he finds them and develops them
in the manner that he has learned from the poets and the mystics. There
is, naturally enough, the vast association between light and the sun,
thence light and the day, and conversely, dark and the night. These
relationships appear throughout the poetry. The terms "sun," "day,"
and "light" are often equated with the meanings of Light as they have
been indicated above. On the other hand, the terms "night" and "dark"
or "shades" and "blackness" are equated with the power of evil and
the lower world, with error and the devil. Spiritual blindness too partakes of the darkness of error. The most important contrasting relationships are those of day/night, light/dark, sight/blindness, life/death, and
white/black. These five distinct antitheses constitute a strong symbolic
group in the poetry and are present everywhere.

The most specific use of uncontrasted light in Crashaw is in the
description of the heavenly regions, the residence of the blest. Heaven
is described in Dantean terms as "the Bright/Regions of peacefull
Light,"[6] as "the originall sourse of LIGHT & intellectuall Day."[7] This
bright light which is the atmosphere of heaven irradiates the inhabitants
who live and bask in its celestial emanations. The Virgin Mary is "attended by such bright/Soules as thy shining self [St. Teresa]."[8] Similarly the angelic hierarchy is vested with this bright light. St. Matthew
reports (28.3) that the countenance of the angel guarding the tomb
on the morning of the Resurrection was like lightning. Crashaw addresses this angel as "bright Sir,"[9] and "The high-born Brood of Day

---

[5] St. Teresa, *The Interior Castle*, I, ii [Peers, II, 205].
[6] Martin, p. 242, ll. 115-116.
[7] *Ibid.*, p. 339, ll. 36-39. The expression "intellectuall Day" appears twice in the poetry.
Here it seems to refer cosmographically to the throne of God; in its other use (p. 326,
l. 97) it would seem to imply the inebriating experience of divine love and favor as
recorded by St. Teresa. Both images suggest that the mystical rapture is intellectual.
See also p. 343, l. 29, and note 60, p. 68.
[8] *Ibid.*, p. 320, ll. 124-125, "Hymn to St. Teresa."
[9] *Ibid.*, p. 87, III; the annunciation angel is "candidus" (p. 57, I).

. . . [as] bright / Candidates of blissefull Light."[10] As the saints mount
to their celestial homes their heads are wreathed by the glory which is
the crown of their labors and good works. The halo which Mary
receives is "the bright / Crown of a most incomparable light."[11] The
writings of St. Teresa, her "larg Books of day,"[12] have gone before
her and in heaven add to her illumination: "[Their] light shall liue
bright in thy FACE / By glory."[13] The divine brightness is not restricted
to the heavenly company; it glows in the lives of those who are led in
the paths of righteousness for His name's sake, since for these God
"Spreads a Path cleare as the Day."[14] These paths of righteousness,
marked off by light like passageways in this blacked-out world, are those
precepts set forth in the Bible that lead to the realm of bliss. They are
the approaches of the stairway to heaven. "Walk with HIM," says the
poet-preacher,

> those wayes of light
> Which who in death would liue to see
> Must learn in life to dy like thee [St. Teresa].[15]

Darkness and its cognate evils are also treated without the contrast
of light and goodness. In his "darke world,"[16] man struggles on the
darkling plain

> Midst all the darke and knotty Snares
> Blacke wit or malice can or dares.[17]

Man's sins are dark,[18] and man himself is one of the "dark Sons of
Dust & Sorrow."[19] Death is "the darke volume of our fate,"[20] and,
in the paraphrase of the Twenty-third Psalm, Crashaw elaborates
theatrically and synesthetically on "the valley of the shadow of death":

[10] *Ibid.*, p. 239, ll. 7-8, "Hymn to the Name of Jesus." It is difficult to guess to whom
Crashaw is referring in this phrase. Strictly, the candidates are the catechumens of the
ancient church, garbed in white until their admisssion to the company of the faithful (*see*
"Catechumen," *Catholic Encyclopedia*): hence, presumably, any persons preparing for
baptism or confirmation. But the symbolic context in which the phrase occurs here suggests
strongly a celestial background.
[11] Martin, p. 306, ll. 60-61.
[12] *Ibid.*, p. 321, l. 88.
[13] *Ibid.*, p. 321, ll. 163-164.
[14] *Ibid.*, p. 103, l. 29.
[15] *Ibid.*, p. 321, ll. 180-182, "Hymn to St. Teresa."
[16] *Ibid.*, p. 140, l. 36; omitted in final version. Doubt is dark; p. 115, xxiv; p. 191,
l. 12, "Isaacsons *Chronologie.*"
[17] *Ibid.*, p. 92, ll. 1-2.
[18] *Ibid.*, p. 137, l. 4.
[19] *Ibid.*, p. 242, l. 99. The phrase occurs also in the paraphrase of Catullus, Carmen
v (p. 194, I), for "nobis cum semel occidit brevis lux."
[20] *Ibid.*, p. 172, l. 41.

> Come now all yee terrors, sally
> Muster forth into the valley,
> Where triumphant darknesse hovers
> With a sable wing, that covers
> Brooding Horror. Come thou Death,
> Let the damps of thy dull Breath
> Overshadow even the shade,
> And make darknesse selfe afraid.[21]

Hell is "the caues of night," [22] and a neat comparison between the darkness of Hell and the darkness of men's souls in this world is given in St. Teresa's comments on sin:

> I doubt though when the World's in Hell,
> It will not love its Darknesse halfe so well.[23]

The "Sospetto" is full of the imagery of darkness. Crashaw depicts Satan, "Father and Heyre of darkenesse," [24] in a rage of passion:

> While new Thoughts boyl'd in his enraged Brest,
> His gloomy Bosomes darkest Character,
> Was in his shady forehead seen exprest.
> The forehead's shade in Griefes expression there,
> Is what in signe of joy among the blest
> The faces lightning, or a smile is here.[25]

One particular use of blackness must be mentioned. In the version of the poem, "On a Treatise of Charity," which appeared in 1635 prefacing the *Five Pious and Learned Discourses* of Robert Shelford, a graduate of Peterhouse, occur the lines:

> . . . *the Pope*: by which black name they call
> The Turk, the Devil, Furies, Hell and all,
> And something more. O he is Antichrist:
> Dout this, and doubt (say they) that Christ is Christ.
> Why, 'tis a point of Faith. What e're it be,
> I'm sure it is no point of Charitie.
> In summe, no longer shall our people hope,
> To be a true Protestant, 's but to hate the Pope.[26]

---

[21] *Ibid.*, p. 103, ll. 35-42; *see* Buffum, *Agrippa d'Aubigné's* Les Tragiques, p. 135.

[22] Martin, p. 299, iv, and p. 119, xxxviii.

[23] *Ibid.*, p. 97, III. This epigram and its Latin counterpart, p. 30, III, paraphrase John 3.19, the comment on Nicodemus.

[24] *Ibid.*, p. 400, l. 77.

[25] *Ibid.*, p. 115, xxv. Crashaw's Satan in the "Sospetto" has often been considered as a source for Milton's figure. Austin Warren, "The Reputation of Crashaw in the . . . Eighteenth Century," SP, XXXI (July 1934), 385-407.

[26] Martin, p. 139 n. The strong anti-Roman feelings of William Crashaw are mirrored in his son's early poems on the Gunpowder Plot, composed before 1630 (p. xcii): "Grow

This passage Crashaw deleted from the poem when it appeared in the collection of 1646. It reveals a tolerance in matters of religion, opposed directly to the preaching of his father, William Crashaw. But it would seem that rather than indicating a turning to Roman Catholicism at this early date, these verses disclose merely a commendable broadness in religious matters not expected in Puritan households of the England of this century.

There is one paradoxical image of darkness which represents the dark as good rather than evil.[27] It has scriptural authority, for the Psalmist often sings of the protection "under the shadow of thy wings" (Psalm 17.8; 36.7; etc.). This benevolent shade covers St. Teresa:

> O banner, thy protecting shade
> Strengthens the feeblest for the strife,
> For thou has turned our death to life,
> And life eternal thou hast made.[28]

Crashaw contributes the image to his paraphrase of the Twenty-third Psalm; the light of divine love and mercy is expressed in terms of shade.

> Still may thy sweet mercy spread
> A shady Arme above my head.[29]

Rather more meaningfully, the poet seeks the protective love of the "sad TREE's shade." [30]

In addition to these free and separate uses of light and darkness and their paradoxical union in the image of protective shade, the concepts and colors combine effectively. The contrast between light and dark in the same image is a frequent poetic device. One particular reference that the balance suggests is that of the old law and the new law. "This new Guest [Christ] . . . new Lawes hath given"; [31] He will elucidate

---

plumpe, leane Death; his Holiness a feast / Hath now præpar'd, & you must be his guest" (p. 387, ll. 1-2). For the violently adverse opinion of Puritans on such tolerance as Shelford and Crashaw advocated, see Warren, pp. 7-8; Martin, pp. 437-438, commentary to this poem; F. E. Barker, "The Religious Poetry of Richard Crashaw," Church Quarterly Review, XCVI (April 1923), 47.

[27] There is still one more concept of darkness expressed by the poets, its illumination. So Vaughan's famous oxymoron, "dazzling darkness" in "The Night." I find no close analogy in Crashaw.

[28] St. Teresa, Poems, XVIII, ll. 1-3, "Cruz, descanso sabroso de mi vida" [Peers, III, 297]. Another with the same image, XIX, l. 5, "En la Cruz està la vida." The image appears in Song of Solomon, 2.3, and is glossed by the Saint in Conceptions of the Love of God, V [Peers, II, 387-390].

[29] Martin, p. 104, ll. 59-60.

[30] Ibid., p. 273, Hymn and Antiphona, "Office of the Holy Cross." For the restorative light of love in the shadow even of St. Peter, see Acts 5.15 and Martin p. 87, I.

[31] Martin, p. 89, I.

the code of Jehovah by revelation of the true Light which is to set
Israel free. In the "Hymn for the Blessed Sacrament," Crashaw sees
the replacing of the old by the new law in the institution of the Holy
Eucharist at the time of the Passover.

> Lo the new LAW of a new LORD
> With a new Lamb blesses the Board.
> The aged Pascha pleads not yeares
> But spyes loue's dawn, & disappeares.
> Types yeild to TRVTHES; shades shrink away;
> And their NIGHT dyes into our Day.[32]

The night of the old law succumbs to the day of Christ. "The people
that walked in darkness have seen a great light; they that dwell in the
shadow of death, upon them hath the light shined" (Isaiah 9.2).

The life of Christ is often depicted in imagery of light and dark.
Crashaw refers to the pain of the Circumcision:

> The day of my darke woes is yet but morne,
> My teares but tender and my death new-borne.[33]

The image unites the elements of light and dark and of life and death.
The color distinction appears in the "day of my darke woes"; the life
and death balance which supplements it, in "death new-borne." St.
John (3.1-21) records the visit Nicodemus made to Christ at night;
Crashaw conceives the conversation as having lasted until sunrise.

> Sol oritur. sed adhuc, & adhuc tamen (o bone) nescis.
> Sol oritur. tecum nox tamen est & adhuc.
>
> Non caeli illa fuit; nox fuit illa tua.[34]

The sun rises, the light comes, but not to Nicodemus. Nicodemus'
failure to comprehend earns for him verses 19-21: "And this is the
condemnation, that light is come into the world, and men loved darkness rather than light, because their deeds were evil. For every one
that doeth evil hateth the light, neither cometh to the light, lest his
deeds should be reproved. But he that doeth truth cometh to the light,
that his deeds may be made manifest that they are wrought in God."
Such spiritual blindness is regularly conceived in the imagery of darkness,[35] as in traditional iconography Synagoga is blindfolded. The sacrifice upon the cross is celebrated in the terms of the light and dark images.

---

[32] *Ibid.*, p. 295, iv.
[33] *Ibid.*, p. 98, ll. 11-12, "Our Lord in His Circumcision."
[34] *Ibid.*, p. 357, IV; p. 30, III, and p. 97, III.
[35] For the contrast of spiritual vision with physical blindness, *see* Martin, pp. 48, V;
69, II. Cf. note 87, 81.

> All hail, fair TREE, . . .
> Who broughtst to light
> Life out of death. Day out of night.[36]

Crashaw describes the Last Judgment naturally in terms of light and dark. The Latter Day (in the harshest line in the corpus) is the day "When Glory's sun faith's shades shall chase."[37] The shades of faith are the dark, imperfect, flat reflections of true Faith; "now we see through a glass darkly." On that day, mankind will be divided; the evildoers will suffer punishment from "those eyes! whose angry light / Must be the day of that dread Night."[38] They will be assigned to perdition. The blessed will "wake into a light, / Whose day shall neuer dy in Night."[39] The deathless day Crashaw found in Revelation 22.5: "And there shall be no night there: and they need no candle, neither light of the sun; for the Lord giveth them light; and they shall reign for ever and ever." A passage from Vaughan is apposite:

> One everlasting *Saboth* there shall runne
> Without *Succession,* and without a *Sunne.*[40]

The sun inheres in the references to day, but the image appears specifically several times. It bears the connotations of light and day already developed: love, divinity, visitation of God, His nearness to His people, revelation, re-creation, and satisfaction. Christ is named "the Sun" as well as "the Son," and here as elsewhere the rhyming play facilitates the use of the image. The Sun is the equivalent of the Son; the Latin poem on the Resurrection glosses this meaning.

> Ex vita (Sol alme) tua vitam omnia sumunt:
> Nil certe, nisi mors, cogitur inde mori.[41]

Through Petrarchan associations, suns are equated with Christ's eyes which stream forth their love, protective care, and influence to the comfort of the sinner:

---

[36] *Ibid.*, p. 266, Antiphona, "Office of the Holy Cross." Often in Crashaw, the rhyming pair facilitates the poetry and the symbolism.

[37] *Ibid.*, p. 293, 1. 55. *See* the quotation above from the "Hymn for the Blessed Sacrament" for a comparable use of "shades."

[38] *Ibid.*, p. 299, ii. The image is not in the Latin hymn.

[39] *Ibid.*, p. 340, ll. 19-20, "An Epitaph upon a Young Married Couple." The 1646 version reads: "Whose day shall never sleepe in Night." The later version is an improvement. Sleep is but a half-death; Crashaw wants the image a permanent one. *See* note 73, p. 72.

[40] Vaughan, "Resurrection and Immortality" [Martin, p. 402]. Cf. also the concluding couplet of "Death. A Dialogue."

[41] Martin, *Crashaw,* p. 42, III. The idea is a commonplace; *see* Albert S. Cook, "Notes on Milton's 'Ode on the Morning of Christ's Nativity,'" *Transactions of the Connecticut Academy of Arts and Sciences,* XV (1909), 333-334.

O loue, I am thy SACRIFICE.
Be still triumphant, blessed eyes.
Still shine on me, fair suns! that I
Still may behold, though still I dy.[42]

These eyes also sustain the natural sun and the stars:

from whose all-chearing Ray
The fair starrs fill their wakefull fires the sun himselfe
drinks Day.[43]

But there are times when the brightness of the sun is too strong for
the image desired. At such times the eyes flash with only the timorous
light of stars.[44] The eyes of Christ and of man are spoken of as stars:
"Tolle oculos, tolle o tecum (tua sydera) nostros" and again: "ecce
oculos (sydera nostra) tuos." [45] The eye of the Virgin is also a star in
a cosmological conceit:

. . . on her lap she casts her humble Eye . . .
The faire starre is well fixt, for where, o where
Could she have fixt it on a fairer Spheare? [46]

There is also the equation of tears and stars: both are light, both
sparkle, both fall, and both reflect the love of the being from which
they issue. The tears of the Magdalene are often like stars.

O 'tis not a Teare,
'Tis a starre about to drop
From thine eye its spheare;
The Sunne will stoope and take it up.
Proud will his sister be to weare
This thine eyes Iewell in her Eare.[47]

The astronomical figure is a favorite with Crashaw, and he enjoys
working with it. The preceding examples have concerned images of
the sun and the stars representing eyes and tears. Stars may also represent saints or mortals touched with a spark of the divine light. The
writings of St. Teresa, full of the light of divine inspiration, reflect that
light. Speaking of the *Vida* and its readers, Crashaw writes

[42] Martin, p. 327, ll. 5-8, "A Song." Note the rhyming pair.
[43] *Ibid.*, p. 267, Hymn, "Office of the Holy Cross." The Latin original has only "lumen
coeli gratum" (William Maskell, *Monumenta Ritualia Ecclesiae Anglicanae*, [Oxford,
1892], III, xi). Cf. note 77, p. 74.
[44] Martin, p. 302, l. 4.
[45] *Ibid.*, p. 363, II; p. 361, IV.
[46] *Ibid.*, p. 89, I, "On the Blessed Virgin's bashfulnesse."
[47] *Ibid.*, p. 84, ii, "The Teare."

> Thy bright
> Life brought them first to kisse the light
> That kindled them to starrs.[48]

Divine inspiration reveals the radiance of the love of God which shines through the lives of the blessed and makes of them sainted stars. They in heaven form a company of the elect who rejoice

> When some new bright Guest
> Takes vp among the starres a room.[49]

The Virgin, the Queen of Heaven, is attended by the train of the blessed and is preeminent among them as "The MOON of maiden starrs."[50] One of the more striking astronomical figures characterizes Crashaw's dilatory patroness, the Countess of Denbigh, and urges her to choose the Roman faith and to abjure the wavering, indecision, and procrastination which she is affecting. She can become fixed and unchangeable: "of a meteor make a starr."[51]

Clouds, mists, and fogs of cosmic and atmospheric conditions suggest another kind of image of darkness.[52] These obfuscations reflect God's shining glory if they are divine, but they cover brightness and conceal the light if they are mortal. Crashaw refers to one metaphoric cloud and to several actual clouds from the Bible. The man born blind receives his sight at the sight of the Son (John 9), as Christ remarks:

> Old clouds of thickest blindnesse fled my sight
> And to my touch darke Eyes did owe the light.[53]

Four clouds that Crashaw has singled out from those in the Bible evidence the love of God towards man. In speaking of Hope, Crashaw alludes to the cloud and the pillar by which Jehovah led the Israelites through the wilderness (Exodus 13.21), the type of Christian Hope:

> Faire cloud of fire, both shade, and light,
> Our life in death, our day in night.[54]

[48] *Ibid.*, p. 321, ll. 175-177, "Hymn to St. Teresa."

[49] *Ibid.*, p. 310, xii, "The Weeper."

[50] *Ibid.*, p. 320, l. 123.

[51] *Ibid.*, p. 237, l. 30, "To the Countess of Denbigh"; these lines do not occur in the final version. Meteors were sublunary, hence their irregularity. *See* Chap. VI, Sec. 8.

[52] Crashaw uses the image in his letter to the Ferrar-Collet family (Martin, p. xxix): "this great black cloud that now blotts ye whole face of our Horison." S. K. Heninger, Jr., *Handbook of Renaissance Meteorology* (Durham, 1960), pp. 50-51, 62-63.

[53] Martin, p. 400, ll. 71-72, "Out of Grotius." The last line yields two readings: eyes did possess their vision; eyes did confess that "I am the light of the world" (John 9.5). The images are in the original: "longa caligo fugit, / Meaeque caecus dexterae debet diem." *See* p. 362, III.

[54] *Ibid.*, p. 143, ll. 15-16, "Hope"; the image is, unfortunately, omitted in the final version. Cf. note 74, p. 73.

Christ after his death is received into Heaven in a cloud (Acts 1.9):

> Nigra! licet nimbos, noctem neque detulit ullam.
> Si noctem non fert, at rapit, ecce, diem.[55]

The cloud that takes up Christ returns with the Holy Ghost (Acts 2.1-4):

> Agnosco. nostros hæc nubes abstulit ignes:
> Hæc nubes in nos jam redit igne pari.[56]

Christ foretells that at His second coming he will appear in a cloud, to Crashaw either the sighs of sinful mankind or the humility of the sun (Luke 21.27):

> Nubem quaeris? erunt nostra (ah!) suspiria nubes
> Aut sol in nubem se dabit ipse tuam.[57]

In addition to the cloud manifestations of divine will and magnificence there are cloud manifestations which proceed from man. These fleshly mists cover the face of light in much the same manner as do the dust clouds blown up from the deserts of mortality. These mortal clouds, for example, in the introductory poem to the "Treatise of Charity," darken the rise of Religion; Crashaw instructs the goddess:

> From th' dawn of thy faire eye-lids wipe away
> Dull mists and melancholy clouds: take day
> And thine owne beames about thee.[58]

The brightness of "day" refers to the perfection of Jesus; the dimming effect of the clouds represents the imperfections of man. The image is finely conceived in the "Sospetto d'Herode"; Satan's intelligence is so much impaired by his fall that he cannot understand

> That hee whom the Sun serves, should faintly peepe
> Through clouds of Infant flesh.[59]

The rational force of the mystical rapture underlies this image:

> A soule whose intelectuall beames
> No mistes doe maske, no lazy steames.[60]

---

[55] *Ibid.*, p. 359, III. The whole epigram is full of white/black contrasts. The cloud, though black, is said to have a breast whiter than the swan.

[56] *Ibid.*, p. 356, IV. This cloud is one of fire not light and dark.

[57] *Ibid.*, p. 36, III. Crashaw cites Luke for this epigram, but he must have been thinking also of Matthew 24.29. The prognostication is repeated in Revelation 1.7.

[58] *Ibid.*, p. 138, ll. 7-9, "On a Treatise of Charity"; the same image in a secular poem, pp. 181-182, ll. 3-4, 31-32.

[59] *Ibid.*, p. 115, xxiii. Crashaw sharpens Marino's "Che'l sommo Sol s'offuschi in picciol velo."

[60] *Ibid.*, p. 157, ll. 31-32, "In praise of *Lessius.*" The anonymous author of "The Preface to the Reader" of *Steps to the Temple* echoes the image (p. 76, ll. 64-65). For later version, p. 343, ll. 29-30.

The "intelectuall beames" are not only the ruling of the passions by the mind which is the lesson of this "Translation of Lessius," they are the brightness of the rational in man, the divinity in him, that in which he approaches nearest to God.

Another contrast in the dichotomy of light and dark which is nicely employed with much the same symbolic effect as that of the clouds of mortal darkness is that of spots, blots, and stains. Mankind is besmirched with these disfigurings, but the heavenly company is without blemish. Christ has an "vnstaind brest," and the Virgin is referred to as "my spottlesse one." [61] The image describes the discoloration of Jesus' feet, darkened by the dust of the road of mortality. Washing Jesus' feet with her tears, Mary Magdalene's "eyes flood lickes his feets faire staine." [62] Pilate washes his hands of Christ's death in a river whose resident nymph, the daughter of an "unstain'd Race," ". . . chides the Hands that stain her." [63] The symbolic significance of the image, as in the case of the mists and clouds, is the darkening effect that these discolorations have upon the pureness of the bright light. Addressing Religion Crashaw says,

> Be what thy beauties, not our blots, have made thee,
> Such as (e're our dark sinnes to dust betray'd thee)
> Heav'n set thee down new drest. [64]

Let Christ in mortal flesh die, and the dye of mortality is washed from dusty man. The water and blood from the side of the crucified Lord, Crashaw writes, "wash't thy stain." [65]

In "The Epiphany Hymn," Crashaw provided a companion poem to his earlier "Nativity Hymn." [66] The "Nativity Hymn" celebrates the birth of Christ and his revelation to the Hebrew people; it does so in a study of white and red nascent imagery. The Circumcision hymn, "New Year's Day," continues the coloring of reds, but before reaching its conclusion, it has begun to look ahead to the "Epiphany Hymn" and its coloring becomes light and dark. The "Epiphany Hymn" combines

[61] *Ibid.*, p. 282, l. 61; p. 304, l. 9.
[62] *Ibid.*, p. 97, I.
[63] *Ibid.*, p. 94, III, ll. 6, 14.
[64] *Ibid.*, p. 137, ll. 3-5, "On a Treatise of Charity."
[65] *Ibid.*, p. 278, ii.
[66] *Ibid.*, pp. 253-261. I have been unable to discover any purpose or pattern in the distribution of the parts among the Kings and the chorus. The unusual pattern in lines 134 to 157 does not reflect any unusual thematic structure. It seems strange, too, that the break before the Close should interrupt a choral section. I have disregarded the "speech prefixes" in quoting. There are a few echoes from the earlier Latin epigram (p. 38, II) in the Hymn, but the parallels are not so striking as are those between the "Nativity Hymn" and its "source" epigram. Cf. also p. 51 and note 100.

the light and dark contrasts noted in this chapter into a well-integrated chiaroscuro displaying the arrival of light on an earth still dark in spite of its brilliant sun. The Epiphany is the second manifestation of Christ. The Messiah comes first to His own people and then to the Gentiles; the three Kings represent all mankind. As Isaiah had foretold: "Gentiles shall come to thy light, and kings to the brightness of thy rising" (60.3); "Kings shall see and arise; princes and they shall worship" (69.7).

The hymn is one of Crashaw's finest poems and will bear scrutiny profitably. Miss Wallerstein has suggested that the "single paradoxical symbol on which the whole poem is built [is] the symbol of the sun in eclipse at the Passion"; Mr. Warren has remarked that "Fundamental to the poem is a contrast of natural and supernatural light." [67] Perhaps even more fundamental than either is the contrast of the light of heaven and the dark of earth. [68] This contrast includes these ideas, subsuming as well the differences between truth and error, Christian and pagan, sight and blindness, life and death, purity and stains — in short, the whole complex of antitheses observed in the preceding pages.

The poem divides into four parts, each of which contains a contribution to the richness of the light/dark imagery. There are also overtones of the white/red contrast, but they are not emphasized in the poem and will be discussed only briefly. The four main sections of the poem are I. The Arrival of the Kings to Worship the New Light (ll. 1-41); II. The Comparison between Paganism and Christianity (42-133); III. The Crucifixion and the Eclipse (134-233); and IV. The Surrender of Paganism (234-254). The poem deals with two events in the life of Christ, using symbols of the conquests of light over dark. Even though the poem is about the Epiphany, the Crucifixion is not so much out of place as would at first appear; "the juxtaposition of the events of the Nativity and Epiphany with those of the Passion, of the Word made manifest with the Word rejected, is traditional and ubiquitous." [69]

The general subject of Section I is the announcement of the Kings that they have journeyed from their east to their west to meet the true East, the dayspring from on high. The journey is a paradox, and the hymn of the Kings is full of other paradoxes and apparent contradictions. It begins with the explanation of a mistake.

[67] Wallerstein, *Richard Crashaw*, p. 144; Warren, p. 148.
[68] Arthur Barker notes that "the sun is symbolic of the son" ("The Pattern of Milton's 'Nativity Ode,'" *University of Toronto Quarterly*, X (January 1941), 176.
[69] Tuve, *George Herbert*, p. 65.

> Bright BABE! Whose awfull beautyes make
> The morn incurr a sweet mistake;
> For whom the' officious heauns deuise
> To disinheritt the sun's rise,
> Delicately to displace
> The Day, & plant it fairer in thy face.   (1-6)

The word "mistake" is one of the keys to the poem; the sun makes a mistake in thinking that its light is of its usual importance this morning. But the heavens have disinherited the sun by the sudden appearance of the older Son. The image of primogeniture yields quickly to one of gardening. The heavens have transplanted the day from its traditional location where its significance depended on the brightness of the natural sun to its new location where its significance depends on the effulgence of the Babe's eyes. The sun will find itself without its expected legacy, the wealth of the earth and the adulation of its devotees. The new day which is to replace the old sun is the new Son, "born KING of loues,/Of lights,/Of ioyes!" (7-9). Jesus is the King of Light, that is, divine Goodness (or Love), which is equated with the atmosphere of Heaven, Joy.

The pagan Kings, "The EAST" (13), have come to seek the new East, to pay their tribute to the new sun-god and to admit their spiritual blindness that it might be fulfilled as it was written by the prophet Isaiah. Crashaw assumes, not unreasonably, that the three Kings were members of a heliolatrous Eastern religion. Such a belief was common in the seventeenth century, and the poet follows the tradition. Lancelot Andrewes, for example, considered the three Kings as Chaldean astrologers or astronomers whose pantheon included the god of the sun.[70] In the Circumcision hymn Crashaw speaks again of the sun-worshiping easterners; the nobler beauty of the infant Christ, he says, shall bereave the sun

> Of all his Easterne Paramours:
> His Persian Lovers all shall leave him,
> And sweare faith to thy sweeter powers.
>
> Nor while they leave him shall they loose the Sunne,
> But in thy fairest eyes find two for one.[71]

The Kings, having seen the star in the east (or "at its rising," a more exact translation) have come west, led by its light to Bethlehem. (This is the only mention of the star in the poem.)

[70] Lancelot Andrewes, *Ninety-six Sermons* (Oxford, 1841), I, 254; Alexander Cruden, *A Complete Concordance to the Holy Scriptures* (New York, 1897), "Sun," p. 592; *Catholic Encyclopedia*, "Babylonia."
[71] Martin, p. 142, ll. 33-38; final couplet omitted in final version (in error?).

We, who strangely went astray,
    Lost in a bright
    Meridian night,
A Darkenes made of too much day,
    Becken'd from farr
    By thy fair starr,
Lo at last haue found our way.
To THEE, thou DAY of night! thou east of west!
Lo we at last haue found the way.
To thee, the world's great vniuersal east.
The Generall & indifferent DAY.

               (15-25)

The paradoxes and oxymorons come thick and fast, but the meaning is clear. The Kings confess that in the darkness of their pagan sun worship they have been going astray even though led by what they thought to be a sure and safe guide, the sun. Their pagan darkness has been the very apex of night, the meridian, or the very noon of night.[72] To the Kings, Christ is the beginning day after their long, dark, pagan night; He is in the east the rising sun whom they have gone west to meet. He is to be the universal Light, the true East for all men; He is a goodness and excellence which shall know no differences, shall be undiffering.[73] This is the meaning of the Epiphany in terms of the light/dark imagery; there is a new light in the earth, its dawn is a true dawn as its light is a true light, it replaces the light of earlier religions and reveals that their light was in fact darkness.

The first section closes (25-41) with a series of antitheses, cosmological and astronomical, including a final example of immense spaciousness in small space: "O little all!" (36).

Section II treats the Comparison between Pagan and Christian religions. Its theme is "no longer"; this is a period of farewell and welcome. The comparison is between natural light, paradoxically dark, and supernatural light.

---

[72] Cf. "the noon of sorrow's night," *ibid.*, p. 270, Hymn. The errors of the three Kings and specifically their westward course to the east appear in Crashaw's "Sospetto" (p. 113, xvii) but not Marino's which has: "Tragge di là da gli odorati Eoi,/L'inclito stuol de' trè presaghi Heroi." Lancelot Andrewes contrasts east and west at length in two sermons (*96 Sermons*, pp. 242-243, 254-255). Praz, *Flaming Heart*, pp. 237-238.

[73] *See* these parallel images: "o ver! o longæ semper seges aurea lucis! / Nocte nec alterna dimidiata dies!" (Martin, p. 50, II); "cheerefull spring, / All the yeare doth sit and sing" (p. 102, ll. 5-6); "a light, / Whose day shall neuer dy in Night" (p. 340, ll. 19-20). Cf. note 24, p. 88.

> To Thee, to Thee
> From him we flee
> From HIM, whom by a more illustrious ly,
> The blindnes of the world did call the eye;
> To HIM, who by These mortall clouds hast made
> Thy self our sun, though thine own shade.[74]
>
> (42-47)

The first "HIM" refers to the sun, traditionally "the eye of day" (so called in line 237 of this hymn). The play on the "blindness" and the "eye" serves to emphasize the darkness of paganism and the all-seeing nature of the new day. Even the word "illustrious" has connotations of light from its Latin original. The second "HIM" is the infant God. The Second Person has put on the darkness of the clouds of mortality and manifests Himself as the infant Messiah. By this action He enlightens mankind but darkens His own nature. (The splendid image of the immortal putting on the clouds of mortality will be recalled from the "Sospetto," stanza xxiii.)

The hymn now turns directly to the comparison between idolatry and Christianity.

> Farewell, the world's false light.
> Farewell, the white
> Ægypt! a long farewell to thee
> Bright IDOL; black IDOLATRY.
> The dire face of inferior DARKNES, kis't
> And courted in the pompous mask of a more specious mist.
>
> (48-53)

The Egyptian god of the sun, Osiris, was often represented wearing the crown of Upper Egypt as a sign of his authority. White was the color of Upper Egypt, and the reference here to "White Ægypt" is more than a loose term describing vaguely the sun-bleached sands of the desert.[75] The adjective is paradoxical, to be sure; it must be taken in conjunction with its parallel, "false," in the preceding line. This idol, bright because it is a sun-god, is another indicator of the darkness of the idolatrous heathen. The "pompous mask" serves to conceal the misty darkness of disbelief and ignorance (obfuscations of mankind)

---

[74] This is as close as Crashaw comes in this poem to the rich symbolic parallel Herbert found between the light of Christ and the cloud that led the Israelites out of Egypt (see Tuve, pp. 51-52).

[75] Sir James G. Frazer, *The Golden Bough* (New York, 1935), Part IV, II, 21 note 1. Grosart commends the adjective (II, lxvi) as "true." Plutarch (*Isis and Osiris*, 359E) reports that the Egyptians thought Horus to be of a white complexion.

inspired by Hell (the inferior darkness) by making outer appearances more pleasing and deceptively alluring.[76] The hypocrisy contained in the word "specious" is elaborated in the following lines:

> Farewell, farewell
> The proud & misplac't gates of hell,
> Pertch't, in the morning's way
> And double-guilded as the doores of DAY.
> The deep hypocrisy of DEATH & NIGHT
> More desperately dark, Because more bright.
>
> (54-59)

The gates of hell are the pagan solar religions; they are placed whither their worship tends, in the east. The speciousness of the old paganism is to make damnation seem pleasant. These religions are not golden, but are gilded, double-gilded in fact, more dangerous and seductive, because more gaudy. They are another sort of "pompous mask." On the other hand, Christ is welcomed for the integrity of His brightness:

> Welcome, the world's sure Way!
> HEAVN's wholsom ray . . .
> The deathles HEIR of all thy FATHER's day!
> Decently Born.
> Embosom'd in a much more Rosy MORN,
> The Blushes of thy All-vnblemish't mother.[77]
>
> (60-67)

Christ, the true heir (cf. line 4), is expressed in terms of light and the day. The color of His mother is a modest blush of red against white. The rosy color of the dawn continues this little splash of reds amid the blacks and whites:

> No more that other
> Aurora shall sett ope
> Her ruby casements, or hereafter hope
> From mortall eyes
> To meet Religious welcomes at her rise.
>
> (68-72)

[76] There is probably a pun intended on "pompous masque"; i.e., a spectacle of elaborate but superficial show. Christ's first appearance on this earth was made before modest scenery.

[77] The image of the Son as the source of the sun is in an early epigram, Martin, p. 44, IV, and in the "Office of the Holy Cross," p. 267, Hymn. "Decently" echoes many rubrics of the Book of Common Prayer describing the order and fitness with which ritual actions must be performed. Christ would have been born in an appropriate manner. "Let all things be done decently and in order" (I Corinthians 14.40). On this subject see Joseph H. Summers, *George Herbert*, pp. 73-76, and Herbert, Chapter XIII "The Parson's Church" in *A Priest to the Temple* [Hutchinson, p. 246].

The pagan dawn worship, like the sun worship, is banished; the light and dark controversy resumes.

> We (Pretious ones!) in you haue won
> A gentler MORN, a iuster sun.
> His superficiall Beames sun-burn't our skin;
>   But left within
> The night & winter still of death & sin.
> Thy softer yet more certaine DARTS
> Spare our eyes, but peirce our HARTS.
>   (73-79)

The external qualities of the pagan religions are emphasized again here. Sun worship, like sunburning, may give the appearance of beauty, but it has a transient effect which is only skin deep. Inside the individual there will still remain, no matter how long he basks in the sun of a pagan faith, the darkness of night and the coldness and harshness of winter. Sunburn leaves as easily as it comes; but the bright beams of Jesus, not so painful as the rays of the false sun, are permanent. The reference in Teresa and Dionysius to the darts of the love of God and His "littleness" which penetrates all substances are apposite here.

The listing of the pagan deities follows:

> The altar-stall'd ox, fatt OSYRIS now
>   With his fair sister cow,
> Shall kick the clouds no more; But lean & tame,
> See his horn'd face, & dy for shame.
> And MITHRA now shall be no name.
>   (97-101)

Osiris and his twin sister and wife, Isis, will no longer be exalted to the heavens. He will recognize the horns of his official headpiece as those of cuckoldry (Isis is said to have been adulterous when she conceived Horus) and die for shame.[78] Mithra the Persians worshiped as the Unconquered Sun. His birth was celebrated on the date of the winter solstice, computed at that time as the twenty-fifth of December. As it is on the winter solstice that the sun begins to resume its power and the days begin to lengthen, the twenty-fifth is the suitable symbolic birthday of the sun. Mithra's festivity on this date was taken over by the Christians as their Christmas about the fourth century.

> It was a custom of the heathen to celebrate on the same twenty-fifth of December the birthday of the Sun, at which

---

[78] Frazer, II, 17. "Altar-stall'd" is another paradox: Osiris converted the altar to an ox's stall; Christ converted an ox's stall to an altar.

they kindled lights in token of festivity. In these solemnities and festivities the Christians also took part. Accordingly when the doctors of the Church perceived that the Christians had a leaning to this festival, they took counsel and resolved that the true Nativity should be solemnized on that day and the festival of the Epiphany on the sixth of January.[79]

That Crashaw knew this tradition may be gathered from another reference to Mithra:

> before the Infant Shrine
> Of my weake feet the Persian Magi lay
> And left their Mithra for my star.[80]

Crashaw in the present poem refers to the gifts of the Kings as the "proud persian spoiles" (80). The allusion to Mithra is extremely appropriate; the Persian god of the Unconquered Sun here surrenders his religious authority, and henceforth, since his birthday is assumed by Christ, he will be not even a name.

> Proud sons of death! that durst compell
> Heau'n it self to find them hell;
> And by strange witt of madnes wrest
> From this world's EAST the other's WEST.
> All-Idolizing wormes! that thus could crowd
> And vrge Their sun into thy cloud;
> Forcing his sometimes eclips'd face to be
> A long deliquium to the light of thee.
> Alas with how much heauyer shade
> The shamefac't lamp hung down his head
>   For that one eclipse he made
>   Then all those he suffered!
> For this he look't so bigg; & euery morn
> With a red face confes't this scorn.
>   (110-123)

The worms of mankind, those symbols of worthlessness and baseness, have attempted to force (from *urgere*) their natural sun into the position of deification in which it can be only the form of a dark cloud, in itself not true, and serving but to obscure the true light. The brightness of the sun, which from time to time suffered the moon to pass between

---

[79] *Ibid.*, I, 304-305, quoting an anonymous Syrian Christian; pp. 301-305, *passim.* *See also* Warren, pp. 148-149.

[80] Martin, p. 399, ll. 36-38, "Out of Grotius"; the original has: "Persa me coluit magus,/ . . ./ Suoque Mithrae praetulit sidus meum."

it and the earth, has been but a long failure of light in the waiting for
the true Son. On one occasion, however, the sun did not suffer an
eclipse but actively made one itself. Ashamed of what evils were being
perpetrated in its name, on the occasion of the coming of the true light,
the sun caused its own eclipse; the consequent darkness exceeded any
previous natural eclipse, so great was the mortification of the penitent.

The second section amplifies the light/dark imagery by specifying the
darkness of pagan sun worship — black idolatory — and points out the
blindness of mankind in venerating a shade or a cloud producing only
a superficial effect. Ashamed at being thus wrongly worshiped, the sun
blushes every morning and weeps tears of dew morning and evening.

The mention of the eclipse at the close of Section II anicipates Section III. This section treats the eclipse of the sun at the Crucifixion
and the consequences of that miraculous action, and it adds this image
of light/dark to the pattern of the poem.[81]

> Time has a day in store
> When this so proudly poor
> And self-oppressed spark [the sun], that has so long
> By the loue-sick world bin made
> Not so much their sun as SHADE,
> Weary of this Glorious wrong
> From them & from himself shall flee
> For shelter to the shadow of thy TREE.
>   (134-141)

This masterful image demands for its comprehension a full knowledge
of the symbolic background. The "day" that is in store is the day of
the Crucifixion when the new light of the love of God will flood the
earth. Compared with this light the sun is but a spark. Indeed, it is
even less bright than a spark, for it has been a deceptive shade serving
darkly as a false god to the pagans. At the time of the redeeming act,
the dark, pagan sun will submit itself to the greater light of the supreme
divinity shining down brilliantly in a protective shade of love from the

---

[81] Crashaw might have noticed the pertinence of the eclipse to the Epiphany in
Southwell's poem, "The Epiphanye" [Grosart, pp. 131-132]. It is no surprise to find
astronomical images common to both poems, but the metaphor of the eclipse is at least
unusual: "Stall was the skye wherein these planettes [Christ and Mary] shynde, / And
want the cloude that did eclipse their rayes; / Yet through this cloude their light did
passage finde, / And percd these sages' harts by secrett waies." Another parallel is noted
in note 88. Crashaw has another eclipse image in the "Sospetto d'Herode" (Martin,
p. 112, x, also p. 16, III); he speaks of the fall of Lucifer, the angel of light, as "one
blacke Eclipse" (the expression is not in the Italian), and addresses the angel as "thou
too selfe-wise/Narcissus? foolish Phaeton? who for all / Thy high-aym'd hopes, gaind'st
but a flaming fall." Even the Christian poet cannot escape worshiping the fallen sun of
classical allusion.

cross. This act of surrender to superior brightness is accomplished by
the performance of the voluntary eclipse, in itself a condensed image of
simultaneous light and dark. "And it was about the sixth hour, and
there was a darkness over all the earth until the ninth hour. And the
sun was darkened, and the veil of the temple was rent in the midst"
(Luke 23. 44-45).

> That dark Day's clear doom shall define
> Whose is the Master FIRE, which sun should shine.
> That sable Iudgment-seat shall by new lawes
> Decide & settle the Great cause
>   Of controuerted light,
> And natur's wrongs rejoyce to doe thee Right.
> That forfeiture of noon to night shall pay
> All the idolatrous thefts done by this night of day;
> And the Great Penitent presse his own pale lipps
> With an elaborate loue-eclipse
>   To which the low world's lawes
>   Shall lend no cause
> Saue those domestick which he borrowes
> From our sins & his own sorrowes.
> Three sad hour's sackcloth then shall show to vs
> His penance, as our fault, conspicuous.[82]
>
>   (144-159)

The judgment seat which is to pass on the superiority of brightness is
the judgment of the Crucifixion, not that of the final day. When the
inferior natural sun has been subjected to a greater authority, it hastily
admits the new king of light by hiding itself in an eclipse. By surrender-
ing its three hours' light from noon to three o'clock and allowing darkness over the earth, the sun pays for all the adulation which in the
perversion of nature has been offered it.

The effects of this miracle occurring at the time of the giving of
new laws are threefold: "The shutting of his eye shall open Theirs"
(163).

The first effect (164-189) is a general one which applies to the sun
worshipers and to the world at large, marked by the third personal
pronoun. The showing forth of the nature of God and the love of the
Son in the darkness of this miraculous day is, in a manner of speaking,
a second Epiphany. Here the appropriateness of the eclipse image in
the hymn on the Epiphany becomes evident. The darkness over the

---

[82] The chronology is wrong, but Crashaw may have been remembering Revelation 6.12:
"and the sun became black as sackcloth of hair."

earth is a light unto the Gentiles and from it all the world learns that truly this is the Son of God. Sir Thomas Browne writes,

> That light appeared at his nativity, and darkness at his death, and yet a light at both; for even that darkness was a light unto the Gentiles, illuminated by that obscurity.[83]

Crashaw says much the same thing poetically of the sun worshipers:

> As by a fair-ey'd fallacy of day
> Miss-ledde before they lost their way,
> So shall they, by the seasonable fright
> Of an vnseasonable night,
> Loosing it once again, stumble'on true LIGHT
> And as before his too-bright eye
> Was Their more blind idolatry,
> So his officious blindnes now shall be
> Their black, but faithfull perspectiue of thee;
>   His new prodigious night,
> Their new & admirable light;
> The supernaturall DAWN of Thy pure day. . . .
> It was their Weaknes woo'd his beauty;
>   But it shall be
> Their wisdome now, as well as duty,
> To'injoy his Blott; & as a large black letter
> Vse it to spell Thy beautyes better;
> And make the night it self their torch to thee.
>   (164-189)

The darkness of the day serves paradoxically as the light to the conversion of the Gentiles. The pagans have been misdirected by the pretty show of a feigned day and a dishonest light. Not knowing the true way they were misled. But now, startled in due time by the very wrongness of this eclipse, they will dutifully turn towards the true light and follow Christ. The sun has been too bright and has sunburnt the outer surfaces of men; it has flourished in the blindness of the earth. Now, by the blinding of itself, which is an office of love and recognition, the sun shows the world that the Messiah is come. Through reading the marvels of this eclipse man shall come to know God aright. This action of darkening introduces the lightening of the new day of Christianity. The eclipse is a miraculous one because it is impossible physically for the sun to be in eclipse at the Easter season, for then the moon is at the full;

---

[83] *Pseudodoxia Epidemica*, V, xxii, 16.

the world can give no laws to explain this supernatural event.[84] The self-blotting of the sun shall serve as a method of writing more clearly and understanding more fully the word of God revealed. The two books of God's plan on earth are adumbrated in the shadow of the sun. The Book of Creation is the method of reading God manifest in the world; the Book of Revelation is the method of knowing God in His great heavenly glory. The image of the eclipsed sun suggests both these lines of approach to the intellect of God.

The second effect of the eclipse (190-219) is the particular, the conversion of Dionysius. In one of his letters Dionysius describes the manner of his miraculous conversion after the attempt to explain the eclipse on philosophic and scientific grounds has failed.

> But let [Appollophanes] disbelieve these things by reason of his ignorance or inexperience. Say to him, however, "What do you affirm concerning the eclipse, which took place at the time of the saving Cross?" For both of us at that time, at Heliopolis, being present, and standing together, saw the moon approaching the sun, to our surprise (for it was not appointed time for conjunction); and again from the ninth hour to the evening, supernaturally placed back again into a line opposite the sun. And remind him also of something further. For he knows that we saw, to our surprise, the contact itself beginning from the east, and going towards the edge of the sun's disc, then receding back, and again, both the contact and the re-clearing, not taking place from the same point, but from that diametrically opposite. So great are the supernatural things of that appointed time, and possible to Christ alone, the Cause of all, Who worketh great things and marvellous, of which there is not number.[85]

Crashaw says of the conversion:

> By the oblique ambush of this close night
>   Couch't in that conscious shade
> The right-ey'd Areopagite
> Shall with a vigorous guesse inuade
> And catche thy quick reflex; and sharply see
>   On this dark Ground
>   To descant THEE.
>
>   (190-196)

---

[84] H. D. A. Major, et al., *The Mission and Message of Jesus* (New York, 1938), p. 193. On "black letter" (l. 187) *see* my "Richard Crashaw and the Little Gidding Bookbinders," *N&Q*, CCI (January 1956), 9-10.

[85] Dionysius, *Letters*, VII, ii [Parker, I, 148-149].

From the lesson which he has learned of the miraculous eclipse and through his spiritual vision, Dionysius, though a pagan and presumably a sun worshiper, can see in the marvel the eternal truth and light and in two puns from music sing the praise of the creator. The fruits of this comprehension and conversion are the mystical doctrine of the *via negativa* by which dark road the divine light may be approached.[86] The goal of the mystical approach is a closer union with Heaven.

> Maintaining t'wixt thy world & ours
> A commerce of contrary powres,
>   A mutuall trade
>   'Twixt sun & SHADE,
> By confederat BLACK & WHITE
> Borrowing day & lending night.
>   (214-219)

The commercial figure demonstrates the union with God in the image of cargoes — of light from heaven to earth, and of dark, the only export available here, from earth to heaven. It was from Christ that man borrowed day, and it is to Christ that man lends all the darkness of his sins.

The third effect (220-233) is the reaction of immediate man — man in the first personal pronoun — to this interplay of light and dark. Crashaw makes the experience private in the figures of the Kings:

> We vow to make braue way
> Vpwards, & presse on for the pure intelligentiall Prey.
>   (222-223)

The business of man on earth is to come to know God aright by the exercise of man's most godlike quality, reason, or by the mystical experience. Both methods lead to admiration of the Supreme Intelligence; absolute Truth is revealed.

The image closing this section derives from the bestiary tradition in paradoxical terms of blinding and dazzling light.

> Now by abased liddes shall learn to be
> Eagles; and shutt our eyes that we may see.[87]
>   (232-233)

[86] Dionysius, *Mystical Theology*, IV, V.

[87] For the significence of the closed eye or blindness as a means to true spiritual vision, cf. line 163 of this poem, note 35, p. 64, and epigrams on St. Paul's blindness in which he beheld the true light, Martin, p. 33, IV, and 60, I: "Te ut possit Paulus cernere, caecus erat." For the image of the eagle *see* Chap. VI, Sec. 1. "The lines cited also suggest the ladder paradox in John of the Cross and Estella, namely that what goes down (the eyelids) really goes up (the eagle)" (Eleanor McCann, *The Influence of the . . . Mystics* [Stanford diss., 1952], p. 143).

Crashaw is asking that we learn from the example of the pagan sun and close our eyes in blindness to this world and the darkness of false religion and idolatry. Then we may mount up with wings as eagles and, seeking the magnificence of the brilliant sun, we shall be newly restored, the film cast from our eyes, and we shall live in contemplation of light and truth. He thus again suggests the sun though he does not mention it specifically.

Section IV (234-254), "The Close," is the summation of the themes which have been mentioned throughout the hymn. The imagery of the conflict between light and dark is stated finally.

> Therefore to THEE & thine Auspitious ray
> (Dread sweet!) lo thus
> At lest by vs,
> The delegated EYE of DAY
> Does first his Scepter, then HIMSELF in solemne
> Tribute pay.
>
> (234-238)

Christ is the auspicious ray of light which represents the love of God streaming down to earth; the eye of day, the natural sun, God's delegate, surrenders itself through the agency of the three Kings, its former devotees.[88] By its symbolic gifts it yields superiority to Jesus and rejoices to do so. For now the sun, too, has seen its insignificance:

> For being show'd by this day's light, how farr
> He is from sun enough to make THY starr,
> His best ambition now, is but to be
> Something a brighter SHADOW [sweet] of thee.[89]
>
> (247-250)

This quatrain expounds the Platonic doctrine hinted in the poem. The sun in the universe shall stand as the embodiment of the Light, that is Goodness, which is in Heaven. The actual reflects the ideal and is the symbol by which and through which man comes to love the magnificence and the providence of the Almighty. The poem closes with an image of the sun which has been carefully withheld that it may have its full effect. Classical allusions are rare in Crashaw; here are the supreme skill and daring inconsistency of an artist in the use of the pagan, heliolatrous word to represent the Christian God, for there is such a

---

[88] Crashaw's sun through the kings "layes down / His gorgeous tire / Of flame & fire, / His glittering ROBE, his sparkling CROWN (ll. 241-244); Southwell's three kings "sett aside . . . Their crownes, their robes, their trayne" (cf. note 81).

[89] For another contrast between the sun and the Son, with mention of Lucifer (note 81), cf. Martin, p. 16, III. The brackets are Crashaw's.

thorough exposition of the Christian background that the word has lost all of its pagan significance and is a general term for the ineffable Light and Good.[90] The sun of this world hopes now only

> on heaun's azure forhead high to stand
> Thy golden index; with a duteous Hand
> Pointing vs Home to our own sun
> The world's & his HYPERION.
>
> (251-254)

[90] Warren (p. 180) has overlooked this "bold correlation of pagan and Christian," but it has few peers.

V. LIQUIDITY

THE TENDENCY of Crashaw's poetry to use images of fluids involves both symbolism and technique. Perhaps there is a relationship: the fluid matter of the images assists the fluid manner of the versification. "All things flow," Mr. Warren succinctly remarks; "Crashaw's imagery runs in streams; the streams run together; image turns into image. His metaphors are sometimes so rapidly juxtaposed as to mix. . . . The effect is often that of phantasmagoria." [1] Crashaw's emphasis on liquids — the Christian religion is well-supplied with them — imposes a fluidity on the technique. The symbolic liquids themselves reflect two other symbolic concepts in the poetry. They are susceptible to quantity and to color. The liquids have meaning in tiny drops and in great quantities: in springs, fountains, rills, rivers, torrents, floods, seas, oceans; in dew, rain, showers, deluge.[2] All of these quantitative nouns describe the abundance of the love and power of God. The poem which most clearly displays the climactic quality of Crashavian abundance is the "Song Upon the Bleeding Crucifix," a poem using liquids as a basic conceit (Chapter II, Section 1). The liquids have colors also, and the colors are generally white and red. So water, tears, dew, and rain are white; [3] blood and wine are red. The white liquids exhibit the qualities of purity and innocence observed in Chapter III; the red liquids, like other red things, glow with the love of God. Red liquids, however, do not by their nature represent the carnality of man's sins.[4] For convenience liquidity will be examined on the basis of this color contrast.

The basic white liquid is water. St. Teresa describes in the *Way of Perfection* three properties of symbolic water; all are represented in Crashaw.[5] The first property is that water satisfies thirst, a function stressed by the topographical background of the Scriptures. Christ is

---

[1] Warren, *Richard Crashaw*, p. 192.

[2] These terms are generally merely intensifiers; they have little specific meaning beyond "great, greater, greatest quantity." "Flood" conveniently rhymes with "blood."

[3] For special effects water can be black; it is so in a storm (Martin, p. 88, IV) and in Hell (p. 120, xliv). Curiously, Crashaw does not treat sweat as a symbolic liquid. "Sweat" refers to drops from heat, overwork, exuding liquids, and to moisture generally.

[4] With one exception that I think of. When wine as strong drink produces "the Teares of wrath and strife," it may be said to be red because of man's sins (*ibid.*, p. 91, III).

[5] St. Teresa, *Way of Perfection*, XIX [Peers, II, 78-82].

the well of living waters,[6] and it is from this well that life-giving water
must be drawn. When the dropsical man is cured of his great thirst
(Luke 14.4), Crashaw imagines that he begins to develop a new thirst
for the divine water. "Fælix o . . . morbus! / Cui *vitæ* ex ipso *fonte*
sititur aqua!"[7] An effective synesthetic image occurs in the "Hymn to
the Name of Jesus":

> Lo how the thirsty Lands
> Gasp for thy Golden Showres![8]

St. Teresa remarks: "Thirst, I think, means the desire for something
which is very necessary for us — so necessary that if we have none of
it we shall die. It is a strange thing that if we have no water we die,
and that we can also lose our lives through having too much of it . . .
if only one could be plunged so deeply into this living water that one's
life would end!"[9] So easily the baroque imagination soars from a drop
to a drowning!

The second property of water is that it cleanses. For Crashaw the
cleansing water is the water of baptism. When Christ was baptised in
Jordan, He cleansed and sanctified the waters of the river that water
might thenceforth be pure enough for baptism.[10] Crashaw comments on
the conversion and baptism of the Ethiopian (Acts 8.27-39):

> Let it no longer be a forlorne hope
> To wash an Æthiope:
> He 's washt, His gloomy skin a peacefull shade
> For his white soul is made.[11]

This facetious epigram balances a poem which is at once symbolic and
political. Popular animosity towards Spain is discredited in the lines:

> Souls are not SPANIARDS too, one freindly floud
> Of BAPTISM blends them all into a blood.[12]

[6] John 4.14; Martin, p. 289, [x].

[7] Martin, p. 50, I. Cf. also p. 21, II, for a comparable epigram. "Then he that hath
the Dropsie . . . is thirstie, and the more he drinketh, the more he thirsteth, and the
more he drinketh, the more he fayleth little and little, & swelleth also" (*Batman vppon
Bartholome*, f. 107ᵛ).

[8] Martin, p. 243, ll. 129-130, "Hymn to the Name of Jesus." Crashaw has been
commended for the originality of this image and the strength of the verb; he has them
in fact from the Prayer Book version of Psalm 143.6. Cf. Sir Edmund Gosse, *Seventeenth
Century Studies* (London, 1885), pp. 158-159.

[9] *Op. cit.*, p. 81.

[10] Cf. note 38, p. 22.

[11] Martin, p. 85, II; Miss Wallerstein (*Richard Crashaw*, p. 62) cites an analogue
from Bauhusius.

[12] Martin, p. 322, ll. 15-16, "Apologie." For the political implications cf. Austin
Warren, "Crashaw's 'Apologie,'" *TLS*, Nov. 16, 1935, p. 746.

The concept of washing and the waters of baptism suggest the more specific image of bathing. The image is fairly common in the secular poems, but it appears rarely in the religious. An example occurs in the "Hymn on the Assumption of the Virgin."

> Live, rosy princesse, Live. And . . . may the best
> Of euerlasting ioyes bath thy white brest.[13]

The bath is both a figure of washing and a description of a state of well-being. In the preceding lines there is no need for absolution of the Virgin, and the emphasis is on the glowing contentedness of the white, joyful atmosphere of heaven.

The third property of water, the most significant to St. Teresa, is that water cools. Paradoxically — and somewhat elliptically — the Saint explains that divine water, instead of tempering, makes the fire of God's love burn more fiercely. "What a marvellous thing it is that, when this fire is strong and fierce and subject to none of the elements, water should make it grow fiercer, and, though its contrary element, should not quench it but only cause it to burn the more!"[14] The reconciliation of these apparently opposing forces lies behind many of Crashaw's contradictory conceits, particularly in "The Weeper."

Though pure water is important to Crashaw, water as tears is even more so. Tears by their whiteness partake of or strive toward heavenly perfection; they are the confession of the sinner's guilt. They must originate in the sinner's awareness of his sin; but when they have done so, they are still worthless, for they are mortal.[15] However, as all things come of God, the tears do have an intrinsic worth. "For the water of genuine tears — that is, tears which come from true prayer — is a good gift from the King of Heaven; it fans the flames [of love] and keeps them alight."[16] Pilate thinks that he has washed his hands of responsibility:

> Thy hands are washt, but o the waters spilt,
> That labour'd to have washt thy guilt:
> The flood, if any can, that can suffice,
> Must have its Fountaine in thine Eyes.[17]

Only Pilate's tears, having their source in his eyes and thence in his soul, can confess his guilt and plead for the remission of his sin. Crashaw

---

[13] Martin, p. 306, ll. 60, 62-63.

[14] *Op. cit., p. 78.* Miss McCann also has noted this parallel (*Influence of the Mystics,* pp. 135-136).

[15] Martin, p. 301, xiv.

[16] St. Teresa, *op. cit.,* p. 79.

[17] Martin, p. 88, I. This epigram answers the question posed in another epigram on Pilate's washing of his hands (p. 94, III).

relates how valuable are the desire and the ability to weep the confession of sins:

> how deare's
> To me my Legacy of Teares!
> I'le weepe, and weepe, and will therefore
> Weepe, 'cause I can weepe no more.[18]

More significant than these tears are those of St. Mary Magdalene. This pattern of the Christian sinner, penitent, and saint was extremely popular in religious poetry of the Counter Reformation. She was "a witness of divine mercy, showing mankind the importance of penitence."[19] In the Scriptures she weeps for the death of her brother, Lazarus (John 11.33), she weeps for her sins when she anoints Christ's feet (Luke 7.38), and she weeps on the Resurrection morning (John 20.11). Medieval hagiology and Renaissance poetry gave her the floods of tears for which she is chiefly now known. In one of the many poems devoted to this Saint,[20] Crashaw describes the anointing of Christ's feet:

> Her eyes flood lickes his feets faire staine,
> Her haires flame lickes up that againe.
> This flame thus quench't hath brighter beames:
> This flood thus stained fairer streames.[21]

The epigram concentrates on the weeping woman rather than on Christ. The flood of her tears, clean as water itself, is paradoxically cleansed by the stains of the dust of mortality on the Lamb's white feet. The fire of her hair is quenched by the water of the tears, but, as St. Teresa indicated, it burns therefore all the more brightly. In the poem "On the wounds of our crucified Lord," Crashaw fuses the weeping at the anointing with the (non-Scriptural) weeping at the cross. The Latin "In die Resurrectionis Dominicae" records the tears at the tomb. But the long poems, the preliminary "The Teare" and the two versions of "The Weeper" (discussed at the end of this chapter), have no local habitation and their tears no particular provocation.

Christ also weeps, though less conspicuously than His faithful follower. He weeps in three epigrams over the fiery destruction of Jerusa-

---

[18] *Ibid.*, p. 95, III.

[19] Helen M. Grath, *Saint Mary Magdalene in Medieval Literature* (Baltimore, 1950), p. 95; *see also* p. 93. The commentary on this saint, and the commentary on the commentary, are immense. *See* particularly Perry J. Powers, "Lope de Vega and *Las Lágrimas de la Madalena,*" *Comparative Literature, VIII* (Fall 1956), 273-292; Warren, *Richard Crashaw*, pp. 134-136. *See also* pp. 39, 44-45, and 98-104.

[20] Martin, pp. 16, III; 17, IV; 28, II; 40, I; 41. IV; 58, I; 67, III; 79; 84; 87, III; 97, I; 99; 307. *See* note 89, p. 101.

[21] Martin, p. 97, I.

lem; there is a close association between tears and fire in two of the three. Crashaw writes of the (non-Scriptural) tears from the cross. Man weeps for his sins; by taking upon Him man's sins, Christ takes also man's tears. But though paradoxically the tears have become Christ's, the cause is always man's.

> ah, mi bone Jesu,
> Si possem lacrymas vel mihi flere meas!
> Flere meas? immo immo tuas. hoc si modo possem:
> Non possem lacrymas non ego flere meas.
> Flere tuas est flere meas. tua lacryma, Christe,
> Est mea. vel lacryma est si tua, causa mea est.[22]

Another white liquid that appears occasionally is dew. This drop-like moisture of the morning or the evening readily becomes tears:

> It was for this the day did rise
> So oft with blubber'd eyes.
> For this the euening wept; and we ne're knew
> But call'd it deaw.[23]

In the dedicatory verses introducing the "Sospetto d'Herode," the poet announces that he will write no more of soft loves and that because of his subject he need not be ashamed of his poem.

> Nor needs my Muse a blush, or these bright Flowers
> Other then what their owne blest beauties bring.
> They were the smiling sons of those sweet Bowers,
> That drinke the deaw of Life, whose deathlesse spring,
> Nor *Sirian* flame, nor *Borean* frost deflowers:
> From whence Heav'n-labouring Bees with busie wing,
> Suck hidden sweets, which well digested proves
> Immortall Hony for the Hive of Loves.[24]

[22] *Ibid.*, p. 353, III, "In lacrymas Christi patientis." *See also* p. 281, ll. 37-38. The tears for Jerusalem: pp. 33, II; 48, III; 359, IV.

[23] *Ibid.*, p. 257, ll. 126-129, "Epiphany Hymn."

[24] *Ibid.*, p. 110, iii. Crashaw translates Marino's "Api ingegnose" as "Heav'n-labouring Bees," at "the Hive of Loves." The flowers are nourished by "il chiaro fonte, / In cui d'acqua vital vena sì beve"; Crashaw adds "the deaw of Life" and gives it a "deathlesse spring." The spring may be the water source, but, by assigning to it the line suggesting deflowering by summer and winter, Crashaw leaves the meaning uncertain.
Batman vppon Bartholome (f. 402) clarifies the activity of the bees: "By wonderfull craft of kinde, Bees arayeth hunnye, that is first made of the dew of the ayre. . . . The heauen giueth Honnie to the aire." Crashaw is also no doubt thinking in terms of the traditional Renaissance conceit of the poet as bee. *See* for another bee-honey conceit, Martin, p. 243, ll. 151-158. "Christ is traditionally honey" (Tuve, *George Herbert*, p. 51). *See also* Wallerstein, p. 91; *Parthenia Sacra*, pp. 59-69; Heninger, *Handbook of Renaissance Meteorology*, pp. 68-69.

Like dew, rain has both naturalistic and symbolic meanings. In general, showers of rain, in that they come from heaven are laden with connotations of grace. "Heav'n's kind showers" [25] are beneficent; the thirsty lands gasp for their life-giving virtue. But the word can lose all of its rain significance in favor of a broad and general interpretation of outpouring. Crashaw sings of the Virgin:

> Thy pretious name shall be
> Thy self to vs; . . .
> All the sweetest showres
> Of our fairest flowres
> Will we strow vpon it.[26]

The basic red liquid is blood, specifically the blood of Christ shed for the redemption of the world at the Circumcision and on the Cross. The redness of the blood symbolizes the great love of God for man; its power is that it can wash pure white those stained red by their own sinfulness. By the final sacrifice on the Cross the life of man becomes a tremendous oxymoron, a life in death, a death in life. Jesus is

> The Name of our New PEACE; our Good:
> Our Blisse: & Supernaturall Blood.[27]

The blood of the Cross is beyond nature; it can work miracles; it can atone for the cumulated sins of all mankind for all time. Crashaw never fears that atonement or propitiation will be exhausted: every least drop is sovereign to cure evil; there will be enough for all. The virtues of the sacrifice are many: the blood is in abundant supply, it washes man clean of sin, it is the death of death.

> When on the crosse, my king did bleed,
> LIFE seem'd to dy, DEATH dy'd indeed.[28]

Its excellence can be measured only in terms of itself.

> O neuer could there be garment too good
> For thee to wear, But this, of thine own Blood.[29]

The virtue of the blood is transferable. Its spirit may be caught and maintained by the sinful for the purpose of showing forth a little of the glory of God.

[25] Martin, p. 349, 1. 34.
[26] *Ibid.*, p. 305, ll. 46-54, "The Assumption".
[27] *Ibid.*, p. 239, ll. 3-4, "Hymn to the Name of Jesus."
[28] *Ibid.*, p. 272, Antiphona, "Office of the Holy Cross."
[29] *Ibid.*, p. 290, II.

> O teach those wounds to bleed
> In me; me, so to read
> This book of loues, thus writ
> In lines of death, my life may coppy it
> With loyall cares.[30]

The blood of St. Teresa is present in her writings; Crashaw exhorts her heart to "Liue here . . . / And bleed & wound; and yeild & conquer still." [31] It is this same magic blood which, spilled from her childish veins, would have seeded Morocco with the love of God.

> So shall she leaue amongst them sown
> Her LORD's Blood; or at lest her own.[32]

The martyrs similarly in their deaths bleed Christ's blood.

The blood of the cross, maintaining its redness, is transmuted into wine. Herbert identifies as Love "that liquour sweet and most divine,/ Which my God feels as bloud; but I, as wine".[33] Crashaw calls it "strong wine of loue!" [34] (the intensifier is typically baroque). He comments on the transubstantiation of the wine of the Eucharist:

> But lest THAT [the Christian Day] dy too, we are bid
> Euer to doe what he once did.
> And by a mindfull, mystick breath
> That we may liue, reuiue his DEATH;
> With a well-bles't bread & wine
> Transsum'd, & taught to turn diuine.[35]

Christ referred to himself as "the true vine, and my father is the husbandman" (John 15.1). Miss Tuve has demonstrated the rich connotative background to this image as she finds it in Herbert.[36] Some of the same interest is present in Crashaw, who points out that it is the business of the husbandman to provide the arbor on which the vine may yield its purple fruit.

---

[30] *Ibid.*, p. 286, vi, "Sancta Maria Dolorum." Cf. note 80, p. 118.

[31] *Ibid.*, p. 326, ll. 79-80, "Flaming Heart." Crashaw imagines the heart of the saint as living in the "conquering leaues" of her books; according to report, the saint's heart was preserved in Spain where it effected many miraculous cures (*see* for example, V. Sackville-West, *The Eagle and the Dove*, pp. 99-100).

[32] Martin, p. 319, ll. 55-56, "Hymn to St. Teresa."

[33] Herbert, "The Agonie" [Hutchinson, p. 37].

[34] Martin, p. 323, l. 31.

[35] *Ibid.*, p. 295, v, "Hymn on the Blessed Sacrament." The succeeding stanzas elaborate the Doctrine of Transubstantiation.

[36] Tuve, pp. 112-117, 59-62.

En serpit tua, purpureo tua palmite vitis
  Serpit, & (ah!) spretis it per humum foliis.
Tu viti succurre tuæ, mi Vinitor ingens:
  Da fulcrum; fulcrum da mihi: quale? *crucem.*[37]

This support the True Vine will embrace as closely as ever classical vine did its elm.[38] Though Christ is traditionally thought of as the cluster, Crashaw applies the term to the Holy Spirit, "cadit *vindemia cœli;* / santaque ab æthereis volvitur uva jugis."[39] Zacchaeus, strange fruit on the sycamore, soon will be a more fitting cluster of the True Vine.[40] Even Caiaphas and Judas confess by their bloodthirstiness that Christ is the Vine.[41]

But Crashaw was not satisfied with a little wine; he must "drinke, and drinke, and doe his worst, / To drowne the wantonnesse of his wild thirst."[42] He must drink himself drunken with the blood-wine of the Messiah. The abundance of wine which the mystic demands is in keeping with his insatiable thirst to express the proliferation of the Creator and the generosity of the Redeemer. The mystical experience of union with the Divine, "sweet inebriated extasy,"[43] St. Teresa describes thus:

> When experiencing this joy, it [the soul] is so deeply inebriated and absorbed that it seems to be beside itself and in a kind of Divine intoxication, knowing not what it is desiring or saying or asking for.[44]

The divine intoxication is secured poetically by images of the drinking cup and the plenitude of wine. The idea goes back to the Twenty-third Psalm: "Calix meus inebrians, quam praeclarus est!" Haymo comments: "Id est potus Dominici sanguinis, 'inebrians,' quia terrenorum facit oblivisci, et etiam vita [*sic*] presentem contemni . . . et ille calix 'quam praeclarus est.' Multum scilicet, quia confert vitam aeternam."[45] Mr. Winters has pointed out the similiarity between the rhythms and meters of the "drinking" passages in the religious poetry and those of

[37] Martin, p. 30, I.
[38] *Ibid.*, p. 41, I.
[39] *Ibid.*, p. 17, V; *see* Tuve, pp. 113-123.
[40] Martin, p. 71, II.
[41] *Ibid.*, p. 356, II.
[42] *Ibid.*, p. 98, III, ll. 7-8. God is conceived as drinking the blood of the Circumcision; in another epigram (p. 53, I), the guests at a New Year's Day party are urged to drink this same blood. Cf. also p. 13, ll. 93-94.
[43] *Ibid.*, p. 399, l. 54. Grotius' Latin text suggests the word: "Undæ liquentis ebrios potus bibit / Galilæa pubes."
[44] St. Teresa, *Conceptions of the Love of God*, IV [Peers, II, 384].
[45] Haymo, *Sermones in Omnes Psalmos, Patrologia Latina*, CXVI, 270. *See also* pp. 14-15 for the abundant cup.

the tavern songs of the Elizabethan and Jacobean period.[46] Whether or
not any such imitation is in the mind of the poet, the expression of the
licentious and wild drinking of the taverns is often as common in the
songs of the cloister as in the songs of the street.

> There are enow, whose draughts (as deep as hell)
> Drink vp al SPAIN in sack. Let my soul swell
> With thee, strong wine of loue! let others swimme
> In puddles; we will pledge this SERAPHIM
> Bowles full of richer blood then blush of grape
> Was euer guilty of, Change we too 'our shape
> (My soul,) Some drink from men to beasts, o then
> Drink we till we proue more, not lesse, then men,
> And turn not beasts, but Angels. Let the king
> Me euer into these his cellars bring
> Where flowes such wine as we can haue of none
> But HIM who trod the wine-presse all alone
> Wine of youth, life, & the sweet Deaths of loue;
> Wine of immortall mixture; which can proue
> It's Tincture from the rosy nectar; wine
> That can exalt weak EARTH; & so refine
> Our dust, that at one draught, mortality
> May drink it self vp, and forget to dy.[47]

These lines concluding the "Apologie" for the Hymn on St. Teresa
form an elaborate and exuberant descant on the passage in the Song of
Solomon to which they allude. The Vulgate translates: "Introduxit me
in cellam vinariam, ordinavit in me charitatem." [48] St. Teresa's com-
mentaries on this verse must certainly have been in Crashaw's mind as
he composed his poem.

> I recall that, as you have heard, the Bride in the *Songs*
> says: "The King brought me (or "put me", I think the
> words are) into the cellar of wine." It does not say that
> she *went*. It also says that she was wandering about in all
> directions seeking her Beloved. This, as I understand it,
> is the cellar where the Lord is pleased to put us, when He
> wills and as He wills. But we cannot enter by any efforts
> of our own; His Majesty must put us right into the centre

[46] Yvor Winters, *In Defense of Reason* (New York, 1947), pp. 131-133.

[47] Martin, p. 323, ll. 29-46. For the importance of the Circe reference, *see* Merritt Y.
Hughes, "Spenser's Acrasia and the Circe of the Renaissance," *Journal of the History of
Ideas,* IV (October 1943), 381-399.

[48] Song of Solomon, 2.4. The important words are lost in the King James Version;
this is one passage where Crashaw was using or remembering another translation,
probably Vulgate or Douai but the same wording is in Coverdale and Geneva.

of our soul, and must enter there Himself; and, in order that He may the better show us His wonders, it is His pleasure that our will, which has entirely surrendered itself to Him, should have no part in this.[49]

"He brought me," she says, "into the cellar of wine; He set in order charity in me." From this I realize the immensity of this favour. For one may be given a larger or a smaller draught, either of a good or of a superior wine, and be to a greater or lesser degree intoxicated and inebriated. And so it is with the Lord's favours. To one He gives but little of the wine of devotion; to another, more; while to another He gives such increase of devotion that He begins to take him out of himself — that is, out of his sensuality — and to lead him away from all earthly things. To others He gives great fervour in His service; to others, good impulses; to others, great charity towards their neighbours; and thus they are so inebriated as not to feel the great trials through which they pass. These words of the Bride, therefore, "He brought me into the cellar", can bear a great many meanings at once, and she may come out from that cellar with immeasurable riches. It would seem that the King desires that there shall be nothing left for Him to give: His will is that she shall drink, and become inebriated with all the wines that are in the storehouse of God. Let her rejoice in those joys; let her marvel at His wonders; let her not fear to lose her life through drinking beyond the capacity of her weak nature; let her die in this paradise of delights. Blessed is the death that brings with it such a life! And this is indeed what it does; for so great are the marvelous things learned by the soul, without its knowing how, that it is beside itself, as the soul itself says in the words: "He set in order charity in me."[50]

Like his saintly predecessor Crashaw could not be content with one draught of superior wine; he must into the cellar. There the vast assortment of unsealed love[51] invites him to take now one kind, now another: wine of youth, wine of life, wine of the death of love, wine of exaltation, wine of refinement, wine of the denial of mortality. It is a rare vinedresser, and rare vines that can produce such an assortment; but Crashaw has already said that God is the vinedresser and that Christ is the

[49] St. Teresa, *Interior Castle*, V, i [Peers, II, 252].
[50] St. Teresa, *Conceptions of the Love of God*, VI [Peers, II, 391].
[51] Cf. Martin, p. 293, l. 54.

vine. Their wine, as the saint and the poet agree, is the wine on which
one is willing to become dead drunk in order to live most gloriously.

> O let me suck the wine
> So long of this chast vine
> Till drunk of the dear wounds, I be
> A lost Thing to the world, as it to me.[52]

The concept and imagery of inebriation merge very easily with those
of erotic love. The fusion has its source in the Song of Solomon and
is traditional with the poets. Crashaw uses erotic imagery consistently
in his poems to St. Teresa and to Mrs. M. R. As often as not he maintains the two kinds of imagery side-by-side:

> By thy larg draughts of intellectuall day,
> And by thy thirsts of loue more large then they;
> By all thy brim-fill'd Bowles of feirce desire
> By thy last Morning's draught of liquid fire;
> By the full kingdome of that finall kisse
> That seiz'd thy parting Soul, & seal'd thee his . . .[53]

The cups of wine are now full of a fierce aphrodisiac passion for the
divine assignation. The erotic image appears without connotations of
inebriation in a figure drawn from the legend of Jove's visitation of
Danae in a shower of gold.

> Lo how the thirsty Lands
> Gasp for thy Golden Showres! with long stretch't Hands.
> Lo how the laboring EARTH
> That hopes to be
> All Heauen by THEE,
> Leapes at thy Birth.[54]

The most striking example of the Godhead as lover is to be found in
the "Ode Prefixed to the Book of Common Prayer" given to Mrs. M. R.
The imagery is entirely and unabashedly sexually exciting, quite in the
convention of divine love poetry of the period and influenced specifically
by Carew's licentious "A Rapture." [55]

---

[52] *Ibid.*, p. 287, xi, "Sancta Maria Dolorum." The Latin has "Fac me plagis vulnerari, /
Cruce hac inebriari / Ob amorem filii." Cf. note 123, p. 125.

[53] *Ibid.*, pp. 326-327, ll. 97-102, "The Flaming Heart." For the "finall kisse," *see*
St. Teresa, *Conceptions of the Love of God*, I, III [Peers, II, 359-364, 377-382].

[54] Martin, p. 243, ll. 129-134, "Hymn to the Name of Jesus." The image reappears
in Crashaw's translation from the *Georgics* (p. 155, ll. 4-9).

[55] A. F. Allison, "Some Influences in Crashaw's Poem 'On a Prayer Booke Sent to
Mrs. M. R.'," *RES*, XXIII (January 1947), 41-42.

O fair, o fortunate! O riche, o dear!
O happy & thrice happy she
    Selected doue
    Who ere she be,
    Whose early loue
    With winged vowes
Makes hast to meet her morning spouse
And close with his immortall kisses.
Happy indeed, who neuer misses
To improue that pretious hour,
    And euery day
    Seize her sweet prey
All fresh & fragrant as he rises
Dropping with a baulmy Showr
A delicious dew of spices;
O let the blissfull heart hold fast
Her heaunly arm-full, she shall tast
At once ten thousand paradises;
    She shall haue power
    To rifle & deflour
The rich & roseall spring of those rare sweets
Which with a swelling bosome there she meets
    Boundles & infinite
    Bottomles treasures
Of pure inebriating pleasures.
Happy proof! she shal discouer
    What ioy, what blisse,
How many Heau'ns at once it is
To haue her GOD become her LOVER.[56]

White and red liquids examined separately in the preceding pages, appear together frequently in contrasting color imagery. Water and wine mix their colors and moistures in the epigrams on the changing of water to wine at the marriage in Cana.[57] The miracle adorned and beautified the human love of the married couple, but their marriage represents typically the mystical union that is betwixt Christ and His Church. The wine is also thus the divine love of the heavenly Bridegroom toward His Saints, and it has the virtue of inebriation.

Another Scriptural episode combines blood with water: "one of the soldiers with a spear pierced his side, and forthwith came thereout blood and water" (John 19.34). Crashaw versifies the episode:

[56] Martin, pp. 330-331, ll. 96-124.
[57] *Ibid.*, p. 399, ll. 52-54.

Lo, how the streames of life, from that full nest
Of loues, thy lord's too liberall brest,
    Flow in an amorous floud
    Of WATER wedding BLOOD.
With these he wash't thy stain, transfer'd thy smart,
And took it home to his own heart.[58]

The question of the nature of the water and blood from Christ's side troubled the patristic commentators for centuries. Certain of the fathers saw in this mixture the institution of the two Sacraments of Baptism and the Eucharist.[59] Crashaw would seem to be following this interpretation: with the water, Christ washed the stain (as He does in Baptism); with the blood, He assumed the sin (as He does in the Eucharist). Herbert in "Holy Baptisme (I)" is in the same tradition.[60] Crashaw treats the incident again in a Latin epigram. Here Christ is represented as a wine cask broached by the spear. The "Vinum . . . amoris" flows; Crashaw fears that the liquor is too strong to drink. But Christ has been provident: "Ecce est, quæ validum diluit, unda, merum."[61]

Tears and blood form yet another color contrast in liquidity. The phrase "thy teares I bleed" occurs in Astrophel and Stella, Sonnet 93, and Vaughan writes "His saving wound / Wept bloud."[62] The contrast was familiar to the Renaissance, and Crashaw but followed in the footsteps of his predecessors. In the Pieta called the "Sancta Maria Dolorum" Crashaw visualizes the Virgin weeping at the foot of the cross and Christ bleeding above her; he remarks the similarity in their actions:

While with a faithfull, mutuall floud
Her eyes bleed TEARES, his wounds weep BLOOD.[63]

There is an equation here which is more than a witty verbal metathesis; the Virgin's tears cannot atone for the sins of the world as blood, but they can demonstrate the whiteness of contrition for the world in general. Similarly, the blood of Christ weeps in white penitence for the

---

[58] *Ibid.*, pp. 277-278, II, ii, "Vexilla Regis." Most of the concepts are present in the second and third verses of the original.

[59] Chrysostom, for example. The point is evidently supported in the Book of Common Prayer (1552 etc.), Prayer before the Immersion which recalls the incident on the cross. But the intent of the Evangelist is simply to indicate the symbolic significance of the death without connotations of Baptismal water (Major, *Mission and Message*, pp. 931-932). St. Thomas Aquinas follows this interpretation: "by the water is denoted the cleansing from sins, which was the effect of Christ's Passion" (*Summa*, Pt. III, Q. lxxiv, Art. 7).

[60] [Hutchinson, pp. 43-44; p. 34, ll. 246-247].

[61] Martin, p.58, ll. 11, 16, "In die Passionis." It is the practice in mass to add to the wine "a little pure and clean water" (Book of Common Prayer [1549]).

[62] Vaughan, "Man's fall, and Recovery" [Martin, p. 412].

[63] Martin, *Crashaw*, p. 285, ii. *See* note 65, p. 114.

red sins of the world which He has assumed. In this situation Crashaw must particularize: he must bring the lesson of the cross home to his own heart: [64]

> And if thou yet (faint soul!) deferr
> To bleed with him, fail not to weep with her.[65]

Two other liquids are balm, or balsam, and nectar. They are both colorless fluids of extreme value and preciousness. There is a tradition of their use in Renaissance poetry. Spenser writes:

> which hauing well vpbound,
> They pourd in soueriane balme, and Nectar good,
> Good both for earthly med'cine, and for heauenly food.[66]

Herbert says:

> There is a balsome, or indeed a bloud,
> Dropping from heav'n, which doth both cleanse and close
> All sorts of wounds, of such strange force it is.[67]

Vaughan also treats of balm:

> He gave his sacred bloud
> By wil our sap, and Cordial; now in this
> Lies such a heav'n of bliss,
> That, who but truly tasts it, no decay
> Can touch him anyway . . .
> Then humbly take
> This balm for souls that ake.[68]

The poets suggest the restorative and medicinal qualities of the balm and the divine nourishment of the nectar. Crashaw combines the liquids in his paraphrase of the Twenty-third Psalm: "there I'le sup/ Balme and Nectar in my Cup." [69] Such is the quenching of thirst in the house of the Lord, but balm is available on earth as well. It is an extract of the "Amber-weeping Tree," [70] a native of the "balme-breathing East," [71] and an attribute of the material of the phoenix' nest.[72] Christ

[64] Mr. Martz has made the same comment (*Poetry of Meditation*, p. 115).
[65] Martin, p. 287, ix.
[66] *Faerie Queene*, III, IV. xl.
[67] "An Offering" [Hutchinson, p. 147].
[68] "The Sap" [Martin, pp. 475-476].
[69] Martin, *Crashaw*, p. 104, ll. 69-70.
[70] *Ibid.*, p. 80, viii, "The Weeper"; omitted in later versions.
[71] *Ibid.*, p. 407, iv.
[72] *Ibid.*, p. 249, l. 31; cf Chap. III. "Balsamum is set before all other smells, and was sometime graunted to but one lands among all lands, that is to wit, *Iudea* . . . The Tree is all medicinable. The chiefe grace thereof and first, is in the iuyce" (*Batman vppon Bartholome*, f. 280ʳ). Crashaw connects balm with the milk and honey of the Promised Land (Martin, p. 113, xiv).

is spoken of twice as raining balmy showers of spices.[73] Blood may be balmy; "Wounds . . . weep / Balsom to heal themselues." [74] Nectar is the drink of the gods. Satan, lamenting in the "Sospetto," confesses that Christ "feeds with Nectar Heav'ns faire family." [75] He feeds them then as on earth His blood, which is "rosy Nectar." [76] Even the name of Jesus is a "Fair flowry name" with "Nectareall Fragrancy." [77]

"The Weeper" assembles in its first twenty-one stanzas many of these liquids in an astonishing stream of baroque extravagance.[78] Professor Praz refers to the poem as a "rosary of epigrams," [79] and his metaphor is echoed in the poem: "Still at each sigh, that is, each stop, / A bead, that is, A TEAR, does drop" (xxiv). Crashaw's image is perhaps musical, but it suggests as well the rosary and, thence, the poem itself. Each stanza is a separate unit of sighing and prayer: a bead of great wit and value; a drop, confining infinite riches in small space; a tear, the white liquid of penitence. The poem thus embraces several of the concepts noted in earlier chapters: it is a poem of abundance, of great power in small particles; it is a poem of color, of the heaven-directed whiteness of contrition; it is a poem of liquids, of the many interrelating white fluids that flow together.

The poem has provoked more critical comment than any other poem of Crashaw's, and much of the criticism of approval — there is perhaps more of disapproval — gathers sources and analogues to the exuberance of its conceits and particularly to the abundance expressed in them.[80] It is enough to say here that the excessiveness of the poem Crashaw would have found in the Bible and in hosts of Renaissance writers: St. Teresa, Marino, Donne, Herbert — to name a few. No increase in the number of analogues will make the poem acceptable to those to whom it is

[73] Martin, p. 244, 1. 169; p. 331, 1. 110.
[74] *Ibid.*, p. 320, 11. 108-109.
[75] *Ibid.*, p. 115, xxii.
[76] *Ibid.*, p. 323, 1. 43. Like His "nectareall" blood, Christ's body is the same on earth as it is in heaven (p. 296, xi; p. 292, Emblem). Cf. 2 Esdras 1.19. In a Latin epigram, "In Spiritus sancti descensum" (pp. 17-18), the tongues of fire are likened to a vintage of wine; the heads of the Apostles glow like "nectareo . . . astro" and with "roseis . . . comis."
[77] *Ibid.*, p. 244, 1. 174; like balm, nectar is associated with honey.
[78] *Ibid.*, pp. 307-315; early version pp. 79-83; related poem "The Teare," pp. 84-85. Crashaw thought so highly of the early version he placed it in first position in his *Steps to the Temple* 1646, 1648). It must therefore be a very important "step." For a discussion of its whiteness, *see* Chap. III; because the liquids dry up after stanza xxi, this can not be a discussion of the entire poem.
[79] Praz, *The Flaming Heart*, pp. 218, 226.
[80] For examples: Martin, pp. 448-449; Praz, pp. 218-231; Martz, *Poetry of Meditation*, pp. 199-203; Stephen Manning, "The Meaning of 'The Weeper,'" *ELH*, XXII (March 1955), 34-47; John Peter, "Crashaw and 'The Weeper,'" *Scrutiny*, XIX (October 1953), 258-273. Arno Esch, *Englische Religiöse Lyrik*, pp. 105-117.

presently not acceptable. The poem is one in a long tradition of Magdalene poems, and it draws on a vast store of convention. Crashaw's version is no more bizarre than the works of many other poets; but, if it does startle, it was meant to startle.

The juxtaposition of convention and surprise may seem strange, but Miss Tuve explains in her *Reading of George Herbert* how the poet can work within his tradition and remain original. Herbert, she demonstrates, achieved his originality by linking superficially discrete items in the convention; [81] Crashaw achieves his by carrying the convention one step further along its logical course. The symbols which Crashaw employs — and it may be well here to interject that their resemblance to words is coincidental — are entirely conventional. They are common to Christian poets: Southwell uses them in his "Mary Magdalene's Tears," as do Herbert and Vaughan in poems on the same subject. All have been examined in the preceding pages.

> Hail, sister springs!
> Parents of syluer-footed rills!
>   Euer bubling things!
>   Thawing crystall! snowy hills,
> Still spending, neuer spent! I mean
> Thy fair eyes, sweet MAGDALENE!
>   (i)

The first stanza, based on the Psalmist's "Rivers of water run down mine eyes" (Psalm 119.136), plunges at once into the concepts of liquidity and abundance. The eyes are "springs"; they are liquid water sources (the nascent image). But they exist not simply but dually; there are two of them. They are then "Parents" (another nascent image) of rills, and the poem flows away from the springs. The rills, like the springs or like the cup overlooking its brim, are bubbling, and they emit their streams permanently and abundantly. Two hard, cold, pure liquids — crystal [82] and snow — "melt away as waters which run continually" (Psalm 58.7); they symbolize the softening and warming of the hard and cold human eye and heart of the sinner turned saint. [83] The change is indicated well in the two nascent images and in the adjective "bubling"; they all testify that true contrition must come from within.

[81] *Op. cit.*, esp. pp. 61-65, 79-80.
[82] Crystal to the seventeenth century was "Ice or snow concreted, and by duration of time, congealed beyond liquation" (*Pseudodoxia Epidemica*, II, i).
[83] For the "cool . . . eye" cf. Martin, p. 94, I.

The first stanza pictures the tears as streams of water having great
value and continuing permanently. Stanzas iv and v liken the tears to
milk, cream, and the supracelestial waters, confirming thus their purity
and permanence and adding divine associations.

> Vpwards thou dost weep.
> Heaun's bosome drinks the gentle stream.
> Where th'milky riuers creep,
> Thine floates aboue; & is the cream.
> Waters aboue th'Heauns, what they be
> We'are taught best by thy TEARES & thee.

> Euery morn from hence
> A brisk Cherub something sippes
> Whose sacred influence
> Addes sweetnes to his sweetest Lippes.
> Then to his musick. And his song
> Tasts of this Breakfast all day long.
>
> (iv, v)

The image of the tear falling upward may be a little startling at first,
but there are two rich symbolic interpretations to the figure. The first
is paradoxical: since Christ's feet actually represent heaven, Mary's tears
in falling on them actually are rising.[84] The second interpretation is
more meaningful. Donne suggests the key in a similar or even more
striking image: "So would her soule, already'in heaven, seeme then / To
clyme by teares, the common staires of men."[85] As Crashaw's poems
were "*Stepps* for happy soules to climbe heaven by,"[86] so were these
rising tears a silver stairway to salvation. For only through an humble
and contrite heart, one which weeps its sins, can the soul of man hope
to reach heaven. Like incense of sacrifice or like prayer, these symbols
of penance rise heavenward in search of forgiveness. The white of the
liquids, milk and cream, signifies the would-be-pure character of the
Weeper. As cream rises to the top of milk, so the tears of the Saint
rise above the Milky Way, being more excellent than it. In such an
exaltation they must flow into and be the same as those waters spoken
of in Genesis 1.6. The puzzle of the nature of these waters was not

[84] The image is a commonplace; *see* Martin, p. 433; Manning, pp. 38-39; Praz, pp.
220-221 n. I do not find the idea repeated in connection with the Magdalene, but
Crashaw has used it thrice in referring to the Virgin. In one epigram (Martin, 89, I;
Latin version, 27, II), Mary's modesty causes her to look down, and there she sees
heaven. In the other epigram (p. 354, V), Christ's modesty has caused Him to come
down so low that the Virgin must look down to heaven.

[85] Donne, "Elegie on the Lady Marckham" [Grierson, I, 281].

[86] Martin, p. 76, l. 48, "Preface to the Reader" of *Steps to the Temple.*

solved in the seventeenth century, but the poet says that something of
that nature may be discovered by the analogy with the tears.[87] As these
heavenly waters can only be of surpassing purity and excellence, so must
the tears of the Magdalene be of supreme merit and value. Far from
learning of the firmamental waters from the tears, one learns of the
tears from the waters.

The "brisk Cherub," after satisfying his own needs, has his godly
errands to run. To welcome new arrivals to the Communion of Saints,
Heaven makes a feast: "Angels with crystall violls come / And draw
from these full eyes of thine / Their master's Water: their own Wine"
(xii).[88] The diction echoes the miracle at the marriage of Cana (John
2.1-11) and suggests the mystical union between Christ and the Magdalene. The wine that comes from the tears is richer than the purple
wine from the natural vine (xi), even though its grape (blushing) is
maiden and modest and has not yet been married to the sun.[89] The
virtue of this remarkable wine is easily explained: Christ's "well-pointed
dart / . . . drest this Vine" (xviii).[90]

> The deaw no more will weep
> The primrose's pale cheek to deck,
> The deaw no more will sleep
> Nuzzel'd in the lilly's neck;
> Much reather would it be thy TEAR,
> And leaue them Both to tremble here.
>
> There's no need at all
> That the balsom-sweating bough [91]
> So coyly should let fall
> His med'cinable teares; for now

[87] St. Thomas Aquinas writes on these waters: "I answer with Augustine that, 'These
words of Scripture have more authority than the most exalted human intellect. Hence,
whatever these waters are, and whatever their mode of existence, we cannot for a moment
doubt that they are there'" (Summa, Pt. I, Q. lxviii, Art. 2). Crashaw refers to them
again (Martin, p. 384, ll. 21-25).

[88] The early version had "Angels with their Bottles come," a closer echo of Psalm 56.8.
The revised image probably depends on Donne (Martin, p. 433). The cherub reappears
in a secular poem, "Musicks Duell" (p. 151, ll. 75-80), engaged in the same activity.
See also Antony and Cleopatra, I. iii. 63.

[89] The image of the grape and her groom, the sun, suggests a parallel relationship
between the Magdalene and her Master, the Son (cf. Martin, p. 16, III). Crashaw
alludes to the human aspect of Christ's love for the Magdalene in three epigrams, pp.
28, II; 67, III; 87, III.

[90] There is a vestigial reference to Mark 12.1 in stanza xviii. The Gospel: "A certain
man planted a vineyard, and set an hedge about it, and digged a place for the winefat
[Vulgate: "fodit lacum"], and built a tower . . ." The poem: "Twas his well-pointed
dart / That digg'd these wells, & drest this Vine." The medieval mind would have
recognized that the tower (Hebrew, migdal) was the Magdalene (Garth, pp. 78-79).
See also Isaiah 5.1-2.

[91] One of the few uses of "sweat"—it refers to the drops exuding from the limb.
The word is used again in stanza xxvii to signify overheating.

> Nature hath learn't to'extract a deaw
> More soueraign & sweet from you.
>
>   (viii, ix)

Stanzas viii and ix compare the tears to dew and balsam, heaven-sent and gracious liquids. For all its divine attributes, the dew would give up its function if it could associate with the Weeper.[92] Balsam, too, the rare and rich fluid, has been superseded as a curative by the tears; its only use now is to comfort itself. The tears assume and surpass the virtues of the two fluids: they are heaven-sent, gracious, medicinable, and restorative.[93]

In stanzas xiv and xv the tears are seen as showers of rain. Like dew, they are heaven-sent, hence gracious; here they add to the attributes of the tears beauty and a background of the kind and faithful spring. The beauty is floral, and the flowers may be specified as the roses of divine love. The rain suggests its opposite, the sunshine; the sunshine suggests fire — rain and fire, the paradoxical union which St. Teresa mentioned:[94]

> But can these fair Flouds be
> Friends with the bosom fires that fill thee
> Can so great flames agree
> Æternall Teares should thus distill thee!
> O flouds, o fires! o suns o showres!
> Mixt & made freinds by loue's sweet powres.
>
>   (xvii)

The stanza recalls the introductory distich—

> Loe where a WOVNDED HEART with Bleeding EYES
>   conspire.
> Is she a FLAMING Fountain or a Weeping fire!—

and effects the reconciliation of the antipathetical elements by "loue's sweet powres." This is the only stanza treating the fire that ought from the epigraph to provide half the poem. The cause of the fire is the "well-pointed dart" of love (xviii), the instrument that transverberated

---

[92] The dew is imaged earlier in stanza vi as the tears of the evening; so in Martin, p. 257, l. 128.

[93] Stanza xi of the 1646 ("The Teare") and 1652 versions has "This watry Blossome of thy Eyne." The 1648 version has "Balsome"; it is almost certainly an error. Though the words are surely Crashavian, Crashaw would hardly have written "watry Balsome."

[94] Manning also has remarked this parallel. See, for a skillful use of the paradox, Southwell, "The Burning Babe" [Grosart, pp. 109-110].

St. Teresa and the poems of Richard Crashaw.[95] But Crashaw is diverted; the dart of love sets the heart on fire and then becomes an agricultural tool (xviii). The reconciliation, however, recalls the epigram on the anointing of Christ's feet which combines fire and water in just this fashion.[96] The Magdalene's hair is imaged as fire, her tears as water; the two are "Mixt & made freinds." The Flaming Heart is not then altogether inappropriate for the Magdalene.

Liquidity has flowed from springs to rills to stream to rivers to showers to rain to floods. It is the sort of climactic expansion remarked in the "Song on the Bleeding Crucifix," though perhaps rather better handled there. It has here one final size:

> And now where're he strayes,
> Among the Galilean mountaines,
> Or more vnwellcome wayes,
> He's follow'd by two faithful fountains;
> Two walking baths; two weeping motions;
> Portable, & compendious oceans.
>
> (xix)

All the various types of moisture are symbolically assumed in the largest body of liquid, the compendious oceans.

In attack and defense of this stanza much has been written. The images were in common symbolic use in the seventeenth century, and Crashaw throughout this poem is writing in symbols, not in words. The fountains suggest that penitence must come from the heart of the sinner; [97] the baths suggest that that penitence goes far toward washing the sinner of his sins; [98] the motions suggest that the sinner must be vigorous and constant in his penance; and the oceans suggest that as man's sins are great, so must his contrition be. The oceans of tears are compendious in that they absorb the many symbolic characteristics of the tears that have been expressed in terms of liquids: they are the results of the conversion of a sinner's heart, they are of great value and permanence, they are heaven-directed and hence heaven-blessed, they are of surpassing purity and excellence, they are dedicated to Christ, they are

---

[95] Especially in the "Hymn to St. Teresa" and the "Flaming Heart." The dart is traditionally associated with St. Teresa, not the Magdalene. *See* Chap. VI, Sec. 2.

[96] Martin, p. 97, I.

[97] Mr. Peter (p. 269) suggests the "fountaines" owe part of their existence to the rhyme. I see it the other way round: the fountains echo Jeremiah 9.1; the "mountains" are less apposite. "The flood, if any can, that can suffice [to wash thy guilt], / Must have its Fountaine in thine Eyes" (Martin, p. 88, I).

[98] I believe that it has not been noted that "bath" occurs uniquely here as a noun; the verb is common in Crashaw, and the noun in other poets.

full of grace and restorative powers. When so much symbolic meaning can be compressed into these extravagant metaphors, the extravagance is justifiable. It is on the symbolic level only that the poem is intended to be read.

VI. Other Symbols and Images

1. Animal Symbolism

THE MOST IMPORTANT of the animal symbols is the Lamb. Christ is the Lamb of God, the New Testament fulfillment of the Old Testament Passover victim.[1] Crashaw uses the word in a nonsymbolic sense to mean a sacrificial animal,[2] but he is more concerned with its Christian significance. In the "Hymn for the Blessed Sacrament" he translates closely Aquinas' typological verses:

> Lo, the full, finall, SACRIFICE
> On which all figures fix't their eyes.
> The ransom'd ISACK, & his ramme;
> The MANNA, & the PASCHAL Lamb.[3]
>
> (xii)

Miss Tuve has pointed out that little Isaac who was to be a sacrificial victim and who carried the wood for his own burnt offering was a type of Christ who was a sacrificial victim and who carried the cross for his own death, and that manna, the heavenly food with which Jehovah fed His children in the desert, was a type of Christ, the heavenly food of the New Covenant.[4] Christ is "The LAMB whom his own loue hath slain,"[5] to be sure, but he is also the Shepherd of the sheep. The relationships between the shepherds who adore the Babe at His Nativity and the Good Shepherd,[6] between their flocks and the Lamb's flocks,

---

[1] Isaiah 53.7; John 1.36. Cruden, *Concordance*, "Lamb," "Passover"; Major, *Mission and Message*, p. 718.

[2] Martin, p. 251, ll. 103-105.

[3] *Ibid.*, p. 296. Crashaw's original: "In figuris praesignatur, / cum Isaac immolatur, / Agnus Paschae deputatur, / Datur manna patribus." *See* 2 Esdras 1.19.

[4] *Reading of George Herbert*, pp. 51, 121-122, 162, 198. One of Miss Tuve's sources for the parallel is a pair of "magnificent and beautiful windows of King's College, Cambridge, . . . which we can be entirely certain Herbert [or Crashaw] himself saw." The richness Herbert found in these parallels fills this stanza of Crashaw's, too, but the thought and words are all Aquinas'. The fascination with typology that inspires, complicates, and enriches many of Herbert's poems does not seem to have been a part of Crashaw's response to his religion.

[5] Martin, p. 279 [viii].

[6] For epigrams on the Good Shepherd, *ibid.*, pp. 70, I (Latin and Greek), 357, V; another allusion, p. 300, viii.

are represented with wit and charm in the Nativity epigram already
noted:

> Quem sic monstrari voluit pastoribus æther,
>   Pastor, an Agnus erat? Pastor, & Agnus erat.
> Ipse Deus cum Pastor erit, quis non erit agnus?
>   Quis non pastor erit, cum Deus Agnus erit? [7]

Crashaw explores other theological implications in later stanzas of the
"Hymn for the Blessed Sacrament."

> IESV MASTER, Iust & true!
> Our FOOD, & faithful SHEPHARD too!
> O by thy self vouchsafe to keep,
> As with thy selfe thou feed'st thy SHEEP. . . .
>
> Coheirs of SAINTS That so all may
> Drink the same wine; and the same WAY.
> Nor change the PASTVRE, but the PLACE
> To feed of THEE in thine own FACE. [8]
>
>   (xiii, xiv)

Crashaw is so intimate with the symbol of the Lamb that he can pun
with it.

> When love of Us call'd Him to see
> If wee'd vouchsafe his company,
> He left his Father's Court, and came
> Lightly as a Lambent Flame,
> Leaping upon the Hills, to be
> The Humble King of You and Me. [9]

The enemy of the lamb is the wolf; Crashaw remembers in two
epigrams Christ's admonition to his disciples (Matthew 10.16), "I send
you forth as sheep in the midst of wolves." Here as elsewhere the wolf
represents man's ravening spirit. [10]

Another symbol for Christ is the eagle. St. Teresa refers to the visit-
ing spouse as an eagle, [11] and Crashaw calls the Infant Christ a young

---

[7] *Ibid.*, p. 355, IV; *see also* note 98, p. 51.

[8] This final quatrain is Crashaw's addition to the Latin; it echoes one of his own
epigrams on John 10. 1-16 (Martin, p. 41, III). Miss McCann notes the pun on
"Pastor" and "pasture" is taken from Luis de Léon (*Influence of the Mystics*, pp. 148-149).

[9] Martin, p. 349, ll. 67-72, *Letter to the Countess of Denbigh.* See my note on this
pun in *Explicator*, VI (1947-1948), #48.

[10] Martin, pp. 354, VI; 358, IV. *See also* p. 281, l. 54.

[11] St. Teresa, *Life*, XX [Peers, I, 120, 130]. Peers' note on a passage in the
Exclamations of the Soul of God (XIV) states that "the royal eagle is a common figure
with the Golden Age mystics" (II, 416).

Eagle.[12] The believer who has taken fire from a reading of St. Teresa's books "feels his warm HEART hatch'd into a nest / Of little EAGLES & young loues, whose high / Flights scorn the lazy dust."[13] The animal lore of the bestiary tradition describes the eagle as having keener sight and as flying higher than other birds;[14] Crashaw thinks of both these attributes in his use of the symbol.[15]

The swan is yet another bird symbolizing Christ. The "last comfortable discourse" of the Messiah to his disciples (John 15-18) is, like the last song of the swan, the sweetest.[16]

> All *Hybla's* honey, all that sweetnesse can
> Flowes in thy Song (o faire, o dying Swan!)[17]

The phoenix, employed frequently in the secular verse to refer to the royal family, appears only occasionally in the religious poetry.[18] This exotic bird was for Crashaw the paragon of animals, and its application as a symbol of Christ is very rich. There can be only one phoenix and only one Christ. The phoenix "passeth all others . . . he is held a sacred bird, dedicated unto the Sunne . . . when he groweth old, . . . he builds himselfe a nest with the twigs and branches of the Canell or Cinamon, and Frankincense trees, and when he hath filled it with all sorts of sweet Aromaticall spices, yeeldeth up his life thereupon. Moreover, of his bones and marrow there breedeth at first as it were a little worme, which afterwards proveth to bee a pretie bird."[19] So is it with Christ. He passeth all others; He is the sign of the sunlight of truth; He chose to be born and to die for mankind and to build His nests in the womb and in the tomb;[20] from His flesh and blood is sprung up His mystical body, the Church.

[12] Martin, p. 108, xii; omitted in final version. The image has overtones of regeneration and rebirth.

[13] *Ibid.*, p. 323, ll. 26-27, "An Apologie." See *Paradise Lost*, IX, 1010, and Southwell, "The Burning Babe" [Grosart, pp. 109-110].

[14] *Batman vppon Bartholome*, ff. 176ᵛ-177ᵛ. For a convenient reference, *see* T. H. White, *The Book of Beasts* (London, 1954), pp. 105-108.

[15] For the image of the mounting and sharp-sighted eagle *see* Isaiah 40.31; St. Teresa; and elsewhere in Crashaw, Martin, p. 191, ll. 9-10. *See also* note 27, p. 38, note 87, p. 81.

[16] *Pseudodoxia Epidemica*, III, xxvii, 1.

[17] Martin, p. 95, IV. The swan, being a white bird, also figures in the color symbolism; *see* note 55, p. 68.

[18] Miss Wallerstein has analyzed images of the phoenix (*Richard Crashaw*, pp. 129-132). For Crashaw's witty and paradoxical poem on the bird, *see* Martin, pp. 224-225, "Phaenicis Genethliacon & Epicedion." *Parthenia Sacra*, pp. 265-269.

[19] Pliny, *Natural History*, X, 2, quoted in Gilbert, *Geographical Dictionary*, pp. 28-29; *see Pseudodoxia*, III xii; *Book of Beasts*, pp. 125-128.

[20] The close association between the Resurrection of Christ and the regeneration of the Phoenix is implicit in the eyewitness account of the death and rebirth of the bird at Easter (*Batman vppon Bartholome*, f. 183). Also cf. Chap. III, and Chap. VI, Sec. 4.

The pelican, a bird as remarkable as the phoenix, appears only once in Crashaw's religious verse, and then in a translation. The Latin hymn of St. Thomas Aquinas, "Ad Sacram Eucharistiam," addresses Christ as "Pie pelicane"; Crashaw translates "O soft self-wounding Pelican!"[21] The pelican "loueth too much her children," for she smites herself in the side to feed her dead nestlings with her blood, "And by vertue of the bloud the birdes that were before dead, quicken againe."[22] Sir Thomas Browne adds: "We may more safely conceive therein some Emblematical than any real Story."[23]

Another symbolic animal is the dove.[24] Crashaw mentions both the dove (pigeon, *columba*) and the turtle (*turtur*) and occasionally distinguishes them. They appear as sacrificial victims in Leviticus 1.14, the burnt offering of the poor, and again as such in Crashaw to represent devotion.[25] The dove traditionally is meek and mild, gentle, void of cunning and deceit; hence, it is a fit symbol for faithful Christians, for the company of Heaven, and for the Virgin.[26] The dove is frequently (but not pre-eminently in Crashaw) the symbol of the Holy Ghost, for traditional Christian art represented the Holy Ghost at the Incarnation in the likeness of a dove and "the Spirit like a dove" descended upon the head of Christ when He was baptized. Crashaw may be thinking of these episodes when he visualizes the name of Jesus coming to earth "upon The snowy DOVE's / Soft Back."[27] The dove combines with the eagle to form a composite symbol; Crashaw exhorts St. Teresa to inspire him "By all the eagle in thee, all the doue."[28] By "eagle," Crashaw intends Christ; by "doue," the Holy Ghost. Both Persons of the Trinity are active in the Saint's books. But the symbols yield other meanings. As the eagle is a fierce, highflying bird and the dove is a

[21] Martin, p. 293, 1. 45. Miss Rosemary Freeman (*English Emblem Books* [London, 1948], p. 146) suggests the figure is "an underlying image" in "Lo, how the streames of life, from that full nest / Of loues, thy lord's too liberall brest, / Flow in an amorous floud / Of WATER wedding BLOOD" (Martin, p. 277, ii).

[22] *Batman vppon Bartholome*, ff. 186ᵛ-187.

[23] *Pseudodoxia*, V, i; *Book of Beasts*, pp. 132-133.

[24] The *Carmen Deo Nostro* prints an emblem containing a dove at the head of the "Hymn to the Name of Jesus" (Martin, p. 239). Praz (*Studies in Seventeenth-Century Imagery* [London, 1939], p. 205) has identified it as a medal of Pope Urban VI. The explanation of the emblem from I. Typotius, *Symbola divina et humana pontificum, imperatorum, regum* (Prague, 1601-03), p. 25, reveals that the emblem has no relevance to the poem and that its presence is probably due to the printer's convenience. *Parthenia Sacra*, pp. 199-210; *Book of Beasts*, pp. 144-146.

[25] *Catholic Encyclopaedia*, "Doves." Martin, p. 139, 1. 47; p. 251, 1. 107.

[26] Martin, p. 330, 1. 98; p. 239, 1. 6; p. 304, 1.14.

[27] *Ibid.*, p. 243, ll. 159-160; *see also* pp. 85, II; 300, 1. 7; 304, 1. 7. St. Thomas Aquinas' gloss on the descent of the Spirit in Mark 1.10 contains much about the dove (*Summa*, Pt. III, Q. xxxix, Art. 6).

[28] Martin, p. 326, 1. 95.

bird of gentleness, the line can signify the love of God revealed in an inspiring fire and a soothing balm.

The turtle in comparison with the dove is generally secular, a bird of "soft loves." Crashaw uses the image secularly to refer to lovers,[29] but he does have religious turtles. Mrs. M. R., to whom Crashaw gave a copy of the Book of Common Prayer, is urged to have pure hands and the eyes "of turtles, chast & true; / Wakefull & wise."[30] The descriptive adjectives are carefully chosen: "The Turtle is a chast Birde . . . For he followeth chastity; and if he leeseth his make, he seekth not côpanye of any other, but goeth alone; and hath minde of the fellowship yᵗ is lost, and groneth alwaye; and loueth and chooseth solitarye place."[31] Having all these virtuous attributes, the Blessed Virgin is named "Mother turtle-doue!"[32]

As the classical goddess of carnal love moved in a chariot drawn by doves, so Crashaw's God of Love "moves / By the'even wings of his own Doves."[33] But wings in general serve as a means to soar to heaven. In singing the praise of the name of Jesus, Crashaw exhorts the soul in exaltation: "Awake & sing / And be All Wing."[34] Similarly, musical instruments playing religious music are wings toward heaven: "Complaining Pipes, & prattling Strings" are the soul's "most certain Wings."[35] Crashaw has a radical image of the bar of the cross as wings: "we may rise / Vpon thy wings, & reach the skyes."[36] The most instructive image of the wing occurs in the last version of the poem Crashaw addressed to the Countess of Denbigh "Against Irresolution and Delay in matters of Religion." Crashaw chides the Countess' delay:

> yea those dull things,
> Whose wayes have least to doe with wings,
> Make wings at least of their own Weight,
> And by their Love controll their Fate.
> So lumpish Steel, untaught to move,
> Learn'd first his Lightnesse by his Love.[37]

[29] *Ibid.*, p. 339, 1. 9.

[30] *Ibid.*, p. 329, ll. 30-31.

[31] *Batman vppon Bartholome*, f. 188 (punctuation mine). St. Thomas has what is virtually a parallel exposition (*Summa*, Pt. III, Q. xxxvii, Art. 3); the continual groaning ("the plaintiveness of their song") represents the mourning of the saints in this life (*wakefull*) (Mark 13. 33-37); the solitariness signifies contemplation (*wise*).

[32] Martin, p. 285, v. The Latin has "fons amoris."

[33] *Ibid.*, p. 349, ll. 53-54; *see also* ll. 45-46.

[34] *Ibid.*, p. 240, ll. 15-16. Tuve, p. 157.

[35] Martin, p. 241, ll. 64-65. The image had occurred also in Herbert, "Church-musick" [Hutchinson, p. 65], and Hooker speaks of sermons "as wings to the soul" (*Laws of Ecclesiastical Polity*, V. xxii. 1).

[36] Martin, p. 267, Antiphona, "Office of the Holy Cross." The image is a commonplace of the emblem tradition.

[37] *Ibid.*, p. 349, ll. 47-52, *Letter to the Countess of Denbigh;* also l. 27.

"Love . . . lends haste to heaviest things," Crashaw observes earlier in the poem, as he refers there and here to the scholastic commonplace that a body showed its love to God most clearly by participation in the function of its most notable characteristic.[38] Thus, steel, since it was heavy, declared its love of God by falling and in this devotion metaphorically sprouted wings that elevated it to God.[39]

2. Fire and the Instruments of Love

Fire as the manifestation of the love of God occurs constantly in the poetry, but Crashaw has versified several Scriptural events or allusions which involve fire in other aspects. Fire in these poems is generally limited in meaning.

The fires of Hell figure largely in the "Sospetto d'Herode." A spark sets the rebelling angels on fire, they suffer with Satan a "flaming fall," they inhabit a "shop of flames." Satan himself fills "a burnisht Throne of Quenchlesse fire" and wears "A gloomy Mantle of darke flames."[40] In the poem "Hope," Jehovah leads the Children of Israel out of captivity by a cloud of fire.[41] The Holy Spirit comes to the earth in fire alighting on the tongues of the Apostles (Acts 2.1-4). Crashaw likens the fire to wine in one epigram,"[42] to lightning for the Jews in another,[43] and in the third turns the episode into a private prayer "Vt mihi sit mea mens ignea, lingua luti."[44] Christ weeps over the forthcoming destruction of Jerusalem by fire, and Crashaw suggests that the flames result from the Jews' scorn of Christ's tears.[45] The Emperor Domitian after several ineffectual attempts to destroy St. John threw him into a cauldron of boiling oil. The saint emerged unscathed and retired to Patmos to write the Revelation.[46] Crashaw sees in John, the disciple whom Jesus loved, the love of God aflame in the world, and asks Domitian good-humoredly if adding oil is the best way to put out a fire.[47]

---

[38] Cf. Basil Willey, *Seventeenth-Century Background* (London, 1942), p. 18.

[39] The leaves and covers of Herbert's *Temple* are also metaphorically wings; *see* my "Richard Crashaw and the Little Gidding Bookbinders," *N&Q*, CCI (January 1956), 9-10.

[40] Martin, pp. 109-126, xii, x, viii, vi, "Sospetto d'Herode." The "flaming fall" and the "shop of flames" are not in the Italian. *See* Praz, *Flaming Heart*, pp. 236-237.

[41] Martin, p. 143, 1. 15 (omitted in final version); *see also* Chap. IV. on clouds. Hope is also a "wise, and well stay'd fire!" (1. 82).

[42] *Ibid.*, p. 17, V; he has Scriptural authority for this, though not the most exalted, Acts 2. 13, 15.

[43] *Ibid.*, p. 45, I.

[44] *Ibid.*, p. 368, II. St. Thomas Aquinas explains why the Holy Spirit descended first as a dove and then as fire (*Summa*, Pt. III, Q. xxxix, Art. 6).

[45] Martin, p. 33, II; *see also* in Chap. V the discussion of tears.

[46] *Catholic Encyclopaedia*, "John the Evangelist," quoting Tertullian, *De Praescriptione Haereticorum*, xxxvi.

[47] Martin, p. 52, I. Crashaw versifies the same episode again (p. 365, I). For John in exile on Patmos, *see* p. 24, II.

The "Hymn of the Church in Meditation of the Day of Judgment" is a translation of Thomas de Celano's "Prosa de Mortuis: Dies Irae, Dies Illa." [48] Fire plays two parts in Crashaw's version: it is the means by which the earth is consumed — "The world in flames shall fly away" (i); and it is the permanent residence of the damned — "The flocks of goates to folds of flame" (xv).

A whimsical epigram combines two of Christ's miraculous cures: those of the feverish woman and the dropsical man (Mark 1.31; Luke 14.4).

> Quippe ignes istos his quam bene mersit in undis!
> Ignibus his illas quam bene vicit aquas! [49]

The conflation of the elements suggests their frequent union in Crashaw, discussed in Chapter V. The Weeper is either a flaming fountain or a weeping fire; the Virgin is "the noblest nest / Both of loue's fires & flouds." [50] As rhyming pairs often influence the sense of Crashaw's verse, so here alliteration has the same effect: fire and flood are yoked together.

Fire represents the love of God. It is omnipresent in Heaven and burns on earth in the hearts of the faithful. Crashaw's *Carmen Deo Nostro* desires "To wound, to burne the hart with heauenly fire," [51] and Crashaw himself dies "in loue's delicious Fire." [52] This fire symbolizing divine love is found in the person of Christ who came "Lightly as a Lambent Flame," in the Virgin, and in the angelic host who are Christ's "own fair sonnes of fire." [53] As "those beauteous ministers of light," the Seraphim "Burn . . . bright, / And bow their flaming heads before thee . . . those euer-wakefull sons of fire / Keep warm thy prayse." [54] On earth the love of God inhabits the heart and makes it "bigge . . . with immortall fire." [55] The martyrs are so much possessed with "That impatient Fire" that they become "flaming-brested Louers." [56] Mrs. M. R. enjoys a love of God characterized by

> Spirituall & soul-peircing glances
> Whose pure & subtil lightning flyes
> Home to the heart, & setts the house on fire
> And melts it down in sweet desire.[57]

[48] *Ibid.*, pp. 298-301. Both fire images are Crashaw's additions to his source.
[49] *Ibid.*, p. 360, IV.
[50] *Ibid.*, p. 285, v.
[51] Thomas Car's prefatory Epigramme (p. 235). If this is Crashaw's avowed purpose in the volume, it makes an interesting contrast to the more pragmatic, less exuberant purpose of the 1646 *Steps to the Temple*: "Stepps *for happy soules to climbe heauen by.*"
[52] *Ibid.*, p. 327, 1. 4.
[53] *Ibid.*, p. 332, 1. 25.
[54] *Ibid.*, pp. 280-281, ll. 21-26. Psalm 104.4: "Who maketh . . . his ministers a flaming fire."
[55] *Ibid.*, p. 337, 1. 22.
[56] *Ibid.*, p. 245, ll. 214, 212.
[57] *Ibid.*, p. 330, ll. 71-74, "Prayer Prefixed to a Prayer Book."

The instruments that communicate the fire of divine love to human beings are in fact the instruments of divine love in medieval mystical writing and of secular love in the Petrarchan tradition. The instrument which is to ravish the heart of Mrs. M. R. is a glance; the weapon is to have its source in the eye of the lover. The glance, furthermore, is to be soul-piercing. The noun and its attribute both suggest the conventional conceit. George Peele expresses the idea perfectly:

> loves dwelling is in ladys eies,
> from whence do glaunce loves pearcing darts
> that mak such holes into our harts.[58]

Though Crashaw had renounced Cupid and all his works in the Preface to the *Epigrammata Sacra* and had replaced the blind bow-boy with the new God of love, he was not unwilling to use the amorous tradition for Christian purposes. The lines "In cicatrices Domini Jesu" treat the wounds of Christ exactly as if they were the weapons of Cupid.

> These the passiue weapons are,
> That made great Loue a man of warre.
> The quiver, that he bore, did bide
> Soe neare, it prov'd his very side.
> In it there sate but one sole dart;
> A peircing one. his peirced heart. . . .
> For bow his vnbent hand did serue,
> Well strung with many a broken nerue.
> Strange the quiuer, bow, & dart!
> A bloody side, & hand, & heart! [59]

Peele suggests that the piercing glances are really darts, and the dart is the most important piercing instrument for Crashaw. It penetrates the heart with the infinite littleness that Dionysius noted. The earliest positively dated poem containing the image of the dart of love piercing the heart is "On a Treatise of Charity" published in 1635; [60] in the later poetry the image is frequent. To the dart Crashaw has added St.

[58] Peele, *Hunting of Cupid* (1591), ll. 18-20. Crashaw's secular poems are of course in the same tradition (Martin, p. 159; p. 188, II, iii).

[59] Martin, p. 381, II. The rhyming pair *dart/heart* is common. The traditional military conceits for the battle of the sexes occur in strategic and tactical terms in Crashaw, but with the religious dimension. The Book of Common Prayer is "loue's great artillery" which comes to defend the fortress of Mrs. M. R.'s breast against her enemies ("Prayer Prefixed to a Prayer-book," p. 328, ll. 11-34). Conversely (and perversely) the Countess of Denbigh is resisting the siege of Christ, her lover; she is admonished in military terms: "This Fort of your fair selfe, if't be not won, / He is repulst indeed; But you'are vndone" (p. 238, ll. 57-68). *See* note 69.

[60] The piercing arrow of the God of love and the wound occur in the address to the reader, "Lectori," of the *Epigrammata Sacra*, p. 13, ll. 89-102.

Teresa's fire of love. The ecstasy in which she embraced this burning, piercing instrument the Saint has vividly described.

> It pleased our Blessed Lord, that I should haue some-times, this following Vision. I saw an Angell very neer me, towards my left side, and he appeared to me, in a Corporeall forme; though yet I am not wont to see anie thing of that kind, but very rarely. . . . He was not great; but rather little; yet withall, he was of very much beautie. His face was so inflamed, that he appeared to be of those most Superiour Angells, who seem to be, all in a fire; and he well might be of them, whome we call *Seraphins*; . . . I saw, that he had a long Dart of gold in his hand; and at the end of the iron below, me thought, there was a little fire; and I conceaued, that he thrust it, some seuerall times, through my verie Hart, after such a manner, as that it passed the verie inwards, of my Bowells; and when he drew it back, me thought, it carried away, as much, as it had touched within me; and left all that, which re-mained, wholy inflamed with a great loue of Almightye God. The paine of it, was so excessiue, that it forced me to utter those groanes; and the suauitie, which that ex-tremitie of paine gaue, was also so very excessiue, that there was no desiring at all, to be ridd of it; nor can the Soule then, receaue anie contentment at all, in lesse, then God Almightie himself.[61]

The aim of the *Carmen Deo Nostro* had been to burn and to wound the heart, and the wounds of love are of almost equal importance with the fiery darts of love. The principal wounds of love are of two kinds. The first wounds are the five wounds which Christ suffered on the cross; they are in the strictest sense the "wounds of love."[62] They are the means of man's salvation.

> Thy blood bids vs be bold.
> Thy Wounds giue vs fair hold. . . .
> Thy Crosse, thy Nature, & thy name
> Aduance our claim.[63]

[61] St. Teresa, *Life*, XXIX [*Flaming Hart* (1642), p. 419]. Crashaw has himself cited this chapter in a marginal note on a manuscript copy of the "Hymn to St. Teresa" (Martin, p. xciii). St. Teresa has a poem on the episode. (III, "Yo toda me entregué y dí" [Peers, III, 282]: "The dart wherewith He wounded me / Was all embarbed round with love." Miss McCann points out that Crashaw's account of the transverberation closely parallels the saint's (McCann, pp. 118-120).

[62] Martin, p. 278, iii.

[63] *Ibid.*, p. 275, Antiphona, "Office of the Holy Cross."

These wounds are most completely explored in the "Sancta Maria Dolorum. . . . A Patheticall descant vpon the deuout Plainsong of *Stabat Mater Dolorosa*." [64] In this translation, Crashaw introduces wounds in almost every stanza. He visualizes Mary before the cross suffering with Christ each of His wounds; her suffering pains Christ more. Hence there is an equal interchange of wounds: his wounds weep, her eyes bleed.[65] Crashaw, standing between the two, hopes to be in Love's way so that

> while the wing'd wounds flee
> So fast 'twixt him & thee,
> My brest may catch the kisse of some kind dart,
> Though as at second hand, from either heart.
>
> O you, your own best Darts
> Dear, dolefull hearts!
> Hail; & strike home & make me see
> That wounded bosomes their own weapons be.
> Come wounds! come darts!
> Nail'd hands! & peirced hearts!
> (vii, viii)

In this poem Crashaw wishes to be identified with Christ "till we mix/ Wounds; and become one crucifix" (x). The two stanzas and the last wish here quoted are original; they have no source in the Latin.

The "wounded bosom" is the second of the wounds of love. It is specifically the transverberation of St. Teresa, but the general spiritual piercing of the heart has affected Mary Magdalene, who also has a wounded heart. It has affected Crashaw, and it may affect the irresolute Countess of Denbigh:

> Meet [loue's] well-meaning Wounds, wise heart!
> And hast to drink the wholsome dart.
> That healing shaft, which heaun till now
> Hath in loue's quiuer hid for you.
> O Dart of loue! arrow of light!
> O happy you, if it hitt right.[66]

The three St. Teresa poems — "The Hymn to St. Teresa," "An Apologie for the Fore-going Hymne," and "The Flaming Heart" — abound with images of the fire of love, the dart of divine penetration,

---

[64] *Ibid.* pp. 283-287.
[65] Mary's participation in Christ's pain is traditional; in compensation, she had an easy parturition (*ibid.*, p. 52, IV; p. 367, II; *Summa*, Pt. III, Q. xxxv, Art. 6).
[66] Martin, p. 237, ll. 45-50, "To the Countess of Denbigh"; omitted in final version.

and the welcome wound caused by the shaft of the seraph.[67] The
"Hymn" gives a summary biography of the Saint's life and explains the
sacred fire with which she burns:

> Love touch't her HEART, & lo it beates
> High, & burnes with such braue heates;
> Such thirsts to dy, as dares drink vp,
> A thousand cold deaths in one cup.
> Good reason. For she breathes All fire.
>
> (ll. 35-39)

This fire she receives from the visit of the fiery seraph who brings Love's
dart to her.

> His is the DART must make the DEATH
> Whose stroke shall tast thy hallow'd breath;
> A Dart thrice dip't in that rich flame
> Which writes thy spouse's radiant Name
> Vpon the roof of Heau'n; . . .
>   So rare,
> So spirituall, pure & fair
> Must be th'immortall instrument
> Vpon whose choice point shall be sent
> A life so lou'd; And that there be
> Fitt executioners for Thee,
> The fair'st & first-born sons of fire
> Blest SERAPHIM, shall leaue their quire
> And turn loue's souldiers, vpon THEE
> To exercise their archerie.
>
> (79-96)

The Saint is thus a "sweet incendiary," and "Her happy fire-works"
are her writings, those volumes which inspired Crashaw.[68] He then has
taken fire from her fire, and in "An Apologie" he admits that in these
poems he transfuses the flame he took from reading her books "back
again to thy bright name / (Fair floud of holy fires!)" (ll. 1-2). The
argument of "The Flaming Heart" is that the illustrations of St. Teresa
"as she is usually expressed with a Seraphim biside her" are erroneous.
She is painted as a weak spiritless female while the seraph is afire with
divine love. The situation must be reversed: the seraph must surrender
his fiery superiority to the Saint with the flaming heart. He has merely

[67] *Ibid.*, pp. 315-327.
[68] "Flaming Heart," ll. 85, 18.

come down from heaven to consult her books. He does not shoot her; she rather in her books sends "A SERAPHIM at euery shott" (l. 54).

> What magazins of immortall ARMES there shine!
> Heaun's great artillery in each loue-spun line.
>   (ll. 55-56)

The painter has erred; he would have painted more appropriately had his "pale-fac't purple took / Fire from the burning cheeks of that bright Booke" (27-28). Corroborating testimony comes from "all ye wise & well-peirc't hearts / That liue & dy amidst her darts" (49-50). Crashaw concludes: "Giue then the dart to her who giues the flame" (57). But, says the poet, if this may not be, he will be content if the painter

> Leaue HER alone THE FLAMING HEART.
>   Leaue her that; & thou shalt leaue her
> Not one loose shaft but loue's whole quiuer.
> For in loue's feild was neuer found
> A nobler weapon than a WOVND.
> Loue's passiues are his actiu'st part.[69]
> The wounded is the wounding heart.
> O HEART! the æquall poise of lou'es both parts
> Bigge alike with wounds & darts.
> Liue in these conquering leaues; liue all the same;
> And walk through all tongues one triumphant FLAME.
>   (68-78)

Like the apostles, St. Teresa has received by fire the Holy Ghost and the gift of tongues, and though she speaks another language, "'tis not spanish, but 'tis heau'n she speaks!"[70]

3. The Crucifixion and the Instruments of Hate

The iconography of the Crucifixion concerns the instruments of the pain which the Redeemer suffered before his death and the promise of salvation made in that death. The pageant of our sin's great sacrifice Crashaw displays in detail with love and care in the "Office of the Holy Cross," "Vexilla Regis," "Charitas Nimia," "Song upon the Bleeding Crucifix," and in several short poems and epigrams;[71] but

---

[69] This line glosses the first line quoted above from "In cicatrices Domini Jesu." The idea comes from the secular tradition; cf. Donne, "The Damp" [Grierson, I, 64].

[70] "Apologie," l. 23; Acts 2.4.

[71] The Hymns of the "Office of the Holy Cross" have a specific Latin original (William Maskell, *Monumenta Ritualia Ecclesiae Anglicanae* [Oxford, 1882], III, x-xviii; F. J. Mone, *Hymni Latini Medii Aevi* [Freiburg, 1853], I, 106-130; T. F. Simmons, *Lay Folks Mass Book*, EETS, No. 71, pp. 81-87, 346-349). The images of the Antiphons all seem to be traditional (cf. Tuve, *passim*; Mone, pp. 131-150).

references to the Passion occur throughout the poetry, for the celebration of the death of the Saviour is of prime importance to the devout.

The pains of the Passion are in true Christian paradox the cause of rejoicing; "Is not the soile a kind one, which returnes / Roses for Thornes?" [72] The thorns of the crown transform wonderfully in the imagery to roses. The roses present a naturalistic contrast to their thorns and symbolically figure the divine love of the Saviour. Christ's wounds are no longer wounds for him, they are medicine for us.

> Quicquid *spina* procax, vel stylo *clavus* acuto,
> Quicquid purpurea scripserat *hasta* nota,
> Vivit adhuc tecum: sed jam tua vulnera non sunt:
> Non, sed vulneribus sunt medicina meis.[73]

Christ "from the nailes & spear / Turn'd the steel point of fear":

> Their vse is chang'd, not lost; and now they moue
> Not stings of wrath, but wounds of loue.[74]

The metaphor of the nails as writing implements reappears in the "Office of the Holy Cross."

> Are NAILES blunt pens of superficiall smart?
> Contempt & scorn can send sure wounds to search
> the inmost Heart.[75]

The nails are painful, but compared to the pains inflicted by the hostility of mankind, they are trivial. The spear is a symbol of the warlike cruelty of men:

> Their deadly hate liues still; & hath
> A wild reserue of wanton wrath;
> Superfluous SPEAR![76]

[72] Martin, p. 290, I; p. 101, ll. 21-24, omitted in final version. Miss Tuve points out in the work of Herbert (pp. 62-63) the relationship between these thorns and the thorns of Genesis 3.18, the first-fruits of the curse, but I note no such rich connotation in Crashaw. Mr. Warren suggests that these may be the thorns among which the seed (the Word) fell in the parable of the Sower, Luke 8.7 (Martin, p. 25, IV; Warren, p. 87).

[73] Martin, p. 28, IV; English version p. 86, V. Another epigram has man's faith as the medicine to heal Christ's wounds (p. 29, II). Cf. also p. 13, ll. 95-102. The instruments of hate distinguished in the text are the most important; a fourth, the scourge (*flagella*), appears in one epigram, "In cicatrices Domini adhuc superstites" (p. 59, I). The comparison with the English epigram of the same title (p. 381, II) is revealing. The Latin includes the figure of the Roman soldier who wounded Christ. Crashaw suggests his position is not enviable. In the English the individual soldier has disappeared; the emphasis is on the conceit of Cupid. *See* Sec. 2.

[74] *Ibid.*, p. 278, iii, "Vexilla Regis" (not in the Latin).

[75] *Ibid.*, p. 270, Hymn. The image is lacking in the Latin original. *See* Herbert, "The Sacrifice," ll. 217-220 [Hutchinson, p. 33].

[76] Martin, p. 273. Hymn. The image is lacking in the Latin original for Evensong, but it is suggested in the Hymn for Nones: "Latus ejus lancea miles perforauit" [Maskell, p. xii].

Like the superficial nails, the superfluous spear adds nothing to the contempt and scorn which Jesus received. "Was ever grief like mine?" [77]

The nails and the spear suggest a series of weapons of which the middle term is missing.[78] The middle term, the sword, however, is provided in the prophecy of Simeon to Mary (Luke 2.35): "Yea, a sword shall pierce through thy own soul also." [79] Crashaw uses the three pointed shafts together in the "Sancta Maria Dolorum" to describe the weapons flying between the Mother and her Son.

> His Nailes write swords in her, which soon her heart
> Payes back, with more then their own smart;
> Her Swords, still growing with his pain,
> Turn Speares, & straight come home again.[80]

The Cross itself figures often in the Passion poetry. It is visually the emblem of a scale: "Euen ballance of both worlds! our world of sin, / And that of grace heaun way'd in Him." [81] It is (in Section 1 of this Chapter) a pair of wings. It is also — as traditionally — a tree. The Cross grows from a bud at the Circumcision to a tree at the Crucifixion.

> These purple buds of blooming death may bee,
> Erst the full stature of a fatall tree.[82]

The poet wishes to take root at the foot of the tree; he urges his reader to graft himself to the Cross that he may grow with it.[83] The Cross is the "sad, sweet Tree," "this painful Tree," the "Tall Tree

[77] This passage, or indeed the entire Office, recalls the spirit of Herbert's "Sacrifice" [Hutchinson, pp. 26-34]; see Tuve, pp. 19-99. Crashaw has generally avoided the paradoxical but significant association between the dart, a pointed instrument moved by love (Sec. 2), and the thorn, nail, and spear, pointed instruments moved by hate. The latter in a profoundly Christian sense are also darts of love.

[78] The same sort of increase in growth exists between the knife of the Circumcision and the spear of the Cross: "This knife may be the speares *Praeludium*" (Martin, p. 99, l. 18, "Our Lord in his Circumcision").

[79] The text is the subject of an epigram, *ibid.*, p. 52, IV.

[80] *Ibid.*, p. 285, iii. The image is not in the Latin. Crashaw has frequently connected nails with writing instruments. So we have nails writing here, nails as blunt pens (p. 270, Hymn), nails writing purple notes (p. 28, IV) or red letters (in the English version, p. 86, V), and, in stanza x of the "Sancta Maria," the torn hands transcribe. Crashaw may have remembered Ecclesiastes 12.11: "The words of the wise are . . . as nails fastened by the masters of assemblies, which are given from one shepherd." There is a pun in the epigram quoted above, "Quicquid spina": "stylo *clavus* acuto." The modifying phrase may mean "with a sharp point" or "in a sharp style." For the usual Latin pun on nail *see* note 101, Sec. 4. For other writings, pp. 282, ll. 58-59; 286, vi; 319, l. 82. Miss Tuve finds a different kind of writing in Herbert (p. 132 and n.).

[81] Martin, p. 278, vi; also p. 273, Antiphona. For parallels to this image (which occurs in the Latin), Tuve, pp. 164-167; Praz, *Studies in Seventeenth-Century Imagery*, p. 138.

[82] Martin, p. 99, ll. 15-16, "Our Lord in his Circumcision." *See* note 78.

[83] *Ibid.*, p. 286, vii, and p. 267, Antiphona; p. 279, vii. For another grafting image, p. 357, I. *See also* note 101 to Sec. 4.

of life." [84] As the tree of life, the Cross recalls the earlier tree in the Garden of Eden. The fruit of that tree brought death into the world and all our woe.

> O dear & sweet Dispute
> 'Twixt death's & Loue's farr different FRVIT!
> Different as farr
> As antidotes & poysons are.
> By that first fatall TREE
> Both life & liberty
> Were sold and slain;
> By this they both look vp, & liue again. [85]

The fruits of this tree are several. The most immediately apparent are those of sorrow and shame. Then mankind is the fruit of the tree; Christ too in a direct sense is the noble fruit of the tree. [86] Finally, the tree's "fair increase [is] / The sinner's pardon & the iust man's peace." [87] In the conquest over death and bondage, damnation and Hell, Christ has secured life and liberty, pardon and peace, the last fruits of the tree.

4. Containers

An earlier chapter examined Crashaw's interest in the paradox that a small unit could exhibit an enormous amount of power, love, or energy. There are several images that pertain to units specifically as containers, suggesting enclosed spaces and their openings: cabinets, beds, rooms and their doors, curtains, and windows. [88] The symbol is one of the nascent symbols, or an opening symbol, as the spaces are generally in the active process of opening or being opened. The image occurs at its simplest level in the drawing of curtains in the morning to greet the sun; "draw the Curtaines, and awake the Sun," says a secular poem. [89] The curtains are transferred from the bed or from the window of the room to the eastern sky at sunrise; "purple pride . . . laces / The crimson curtains" of the sun's bed. [90] The sunrise forms the ruby portals

[84] *Ibid.*, p. 273, Antiphona; p. 277, i; p. 278, iv.

[85] *Ibid.*, p. 270, Antiphona. For the relationships between these trees and their fruits, *see* Tuve, pp. 81-86.

[86] Martin, p. 270, Hymn; 266, Antiphona; 279, vii.

[87] *Ibid.*, p. 279, vii. The lines were added after the 1648 publication of the poem.

[88] There is a special "container" that deserves at least footnote notice, prison. Christ's death released the captive world from prison and bound the jailer (Martin, p. 269, Antiphona). Crashaw has also a fine image of a frozen river: "Poor waters their owne prisoners be" (p. 237, ll. 21-24). A parallel image occurs in Phineas Fletcher's *Locusts* (Apollyonists), III, 5.

[89] Martin, p. 183, III, l. 10.

[90] *Ibid.*, p. 251, ll. 5-6; *see also* ll. 17-18. Psalm 104. 2: "who stretchest out the heavens like a curtain."

of the East.[91] The image gains yet more meaning when the curtains
are again transferred, this time to the eyes of a waiting, hopeful world:

> O see, the WEARY liddes of wakefull Hope
> (LOVE's Eastern windows) All wide ope
> With Curtains drawn,
> To catch The Day-break of thy DAWN.[92]

Crashaw wishes to let the dead sleep

> Till th'Æternall morrow dawn;
> Then the curtaines will be drawn.[93]

Though there are no curtains in the next quotation, the association with
the dawn and the opening of doors and windows links the passage to
the preceding ones. The weapons of the Roman persecutors, wounding
the martyrs,

> sett wide the Doores
> For Thee: Fair, purple Doores, of loue's deuising;
> The Ruby windowes which inrich't the EAST
> Of Thy so oft repeated Rising.[94]

There are also images of cabinets or chests for parts of the body.
Eyes, which already have been curtained windows, are also "weeping
gates" and "Caskets, of which Heaven keeps the Keyes." [95] The heart
of the Countess of Denbigh is locked against Christ; He is urged to

> Choose out that sure decisiue dart
> Which has the Key of this close heart,
> Knowes all the corners of't, & can controul
> The self-shutt cabinet of an vnsearcht soul.[96]

Heaven has the keys to these hearts and presumably has authority to
enter the recesses, but when the young Teresa is on her way to the
Moors and martyrdom, Crashaw warns her lest "some base hand haue
power to race / Thy Brest's chast cabinet, & vncase / A soul." [97]

---

[91] *Ibid.*, p. 113, xvi, and cf. p. 256, ll. 69-70. *See also* the general discussion of the
dawn in Chap. III.

[92] *Ibid.*, p. 243, ll. 145-148, "Hymn to the Name of Jesus." The image reflects
Psalm 130. 5-6 (King James). *See also* p. 380, ll. 33-34.

[93] *Ibid.*, p. 340, ll. 17-18, "Epitaph on a Young Couple."

[94] *Ibid.*, p. 245, ll. 216-219, "Hymn to the Name of Jesus." Shakespeare likens wounds
to windows, *Richard III*, I.ii.12. Crashaw likens wounds to eyes to windows, p. 43, I.

[95] Martin, p. 313, xxv; p. 80, viii, omitted in final version. For a secular parallel, cf.
p. 176, l. 25.

[96] *Ibid.*, p. 237, ll. 33-36, "To the Countess of Denbigh," omitted in final version.
Before Christ freed man, Satan inhabited man's breast, "his tenement" (p. 400, l. 80).

[97] *Ibid.*, pp. 318-319, ll. 71-73.

The image has a particularly rich treatment in representing the body of Christ. The Name of Jesus has a "Cabinet of DAY" which it is urged to unlock; it is a hive where all the hoard of honey lies.[98] Christ's body is a container in the epigram "Vpon the Body of our Blessed Lord, Naked and Bloody."

> They'haue left thee naked, LORD, O that they had!
> This garment too I would they had deny'd.
> Thee with thy self they haue too richly clad;
> Opening the purple wardrobe in thy side.[99]

The image is rich in meaning. Purple is the color of blood, of death, of royalty, and of great richness. The wardrobe is the closet for the valuable and lavish clothing of the blood.[100] By opening the door in the body of Christ, there is let out the red splendor of salvation; Christ is dressed gloriously as for a sacrifice. Christ had said, "I am the door: by me if any man enter in, he shall be saved and shall go in and out, and shall find pasture" (John 10.9). Crashaw comments on these lines, considering the fate of the soldier with the spear that pierced Christ's side.

> And now th'art set wide ope, The Speare's sad Art,
> Lo! hath unlockt thee at the very Heart:
> Hee to himselfe (I fear the worst)
> And his owne hope
> Hath *shut* these Doores of Heaven, that durst
> Thus set them *ope*.[101]

The womb of Mary is — in a special sense — another container. Mary's womb is symbolized vividly as the "world's new eastern win-

[98] *Ibid.*, p. 242, l. 127; p. 243, ll. 151-158. The cabinet of day is copied by Satan who has double-gilded the gates of Hell so that they resemble the doors of day (p. 255, l. 57). The cabinet image is a commonplace (Tuve, pp. 140-144).

[99] Martin, p. 290, II. Blood is seen as a garment again, p. 293, l. 25; and flesh is the garment of the soul, p. 343, ll. 19-22. Donne writes: "So in his purple wrapp'd receive mee Lord" ("Hymne to God my God" [Grierson, I, 369]). Herbert's "Sacrifice," ll. 157-160 [Hutchinson, p. 31], has a comparable sentence. Cf. Robert Martin Adams, "Taste and Bad Taste in Metaphysical Poetry," *Hudson Review*, VIII (Spring 1956), 67.

[100] Spenser speaks of Mary's womb as "the deare closet of her painefull side" (*Faerie Queene*, III.II.xi); Southwell has the same image, "Synne's Heavy Load" [Grosart, p. 106]; as does Herbert, "thou hast wept such store [of bloud]/ That all thy body was one doore," "The Thanksgiving" [Hutchinson, p. 35]). *See also* A. Alvarez, *School of Donne* (London, 1961), pp. 99-101; Tuve, pp. 59-60, 129-130.

[101] Martin, p. 90, III. The Latin version of this poem (p. 357, II) has a line omitted in the English: "Et clavi claves undique te reserant." The play is on "clavi" *nails* and "claves" *keys*, though the appositive construction is not the smoothest. Crashaw did manage the pun deftly in the "Office of the Holy Cross": "the dear NAILES did lock / And graft into thy gracious Stock/ The hope [of the WORLD]" (p. 273, Antiphon). The image is one of agriculture also.

dow." [102] The image contains the connotations of the wealth of the east
and of the dawning of a new day. This is the womb with the open
window; there is also a womb with a closed door. Crashaw addresses
Mary:

> Hail, door of life: & sourse of day!
> The door was shutt, the fountain seal'd;
> Yet LIGHT was seen & LIFE reueald.
> The door was shutt, yet let in day,
> The fountain seald, yet life found way.[103]

In Christ's birth the virginity of His mother remained inviolate. St.
Thomas explains: "We must assert that the Mother of Christ was a
virgin even in His Birth: for the prophet says not only: 'Behold, a virgin
shall conceive,' but adds, 'and shall bear a son.'" [104] The authority for
the doctrine is to be found in Ezekiel 44.2:

> This gate shall be shut, it shall not be opened, and no man
> shall pass through it; because the Lord the God of Israel
> hath entered in by it, therefore it shall be shut.

St. Augustine queries:

> What means this closed gate in the House of the Lord,
> except that Mary is to be ever inviolate? . . . Mary is a
> virgin before His Birth, a virgin in His Birth, and a virgin
> after His Birth.[105]

The womb is balanced by another container, which most conveniently
rhymes with it, the tomb. The two containers work together effectively,
for the paradox plays them against each other and heightens their symbolic meanings. The womb is the beginning of the life of God with
men; the tomb is the beginning of the life of men with God.

> How life & death in Thee
>   Agree!
> Thou hadst a virgin womb,
>   And tomb.

---

[102] *Ibid.*, p. 303, 1. 19; *see also* 1. 21. Cf. note 100. The Latin has "coeli fenestra
facta es."

[103] *Ibid.*, p. 303, ll. 32-36. The Latin has "Tu regis alti janua / et porta lucis fulgida."
The next to the last line is omitted in the final version, presumably through error. The
door image of the Immaculate Birth recalls to the Scholastic mind the entry of the
Risen Lord through a closed door (John 20. 19, 26). Accordingly Augustine says
[of the miracle in John] . . . "Closed doors were no obstacle to the substance of a
Body wherein was the Godhead; for truly He could enter in by doors not open, in
whose Birth His mother's virginity remained inviolate" (St. Thomas Aquinas, *Summa*, Pt.
III, Q. liv, Art. 1. *See also* Pt. III sup., Q. lxxxiii, Art 2).

[104] *Summa*, Pt. III, Q. xxviii, Art. 2.

[105] *De Annunciatione Dominae*, III, quoted in *Summa*, Pt. III, Q. xxviii, Art. 3.

> A IOSEPH did betroth
> Them both.[106]

A neat and witty epigram is this, but one which nevertheless catches
the spirit of the similarity of the birth and death of Jesus, expanded
more meaningfully in the epigram, "Easter Day."

> Rise, Heire of fresh Eternity,
> From thy Virgin Tombe:
> Rise mighty man of wonders, and thy world with thee
> Thy Tombe, the universall East,
> Natures new wombe,
> Thy Tombe, faire immortalities perfumed Nest.[107]

The tomb of Joseph of Arimathea is "the universall East," that is, the
opening and beginning place of all things. The phrase has already been
applied in the Epiphany Hymn to Christ himself, "the world's great
vniuersal east" (l. 24), whom the Magi have come to see. As the
womb was the dawn so the tomb may be the dawn, for it is the beginning place of immortal life.

5. Protection and Nourishment

Crashaw's Mariolatry carried him naturally to the source of infantile
protection and nourishment. Having lost his mother and stepmother
early in life, he extended all his normal affection for a mother to his
"mother" at Little Gidding,[108] to St. Teresa, and to his Mother in
Christ. Consequently it is not surprising to find in the imagery an
emphasis on the figures of the nest and the breast. This rhyming pair
is frequently used in a conjunction which tends to equate the distinctive
meanings of the components.

The nest is generally a place of protection and complete satisfaction.
It may also be a beginning place in a nascent symbol. Heaven is a
"Gorgeous Nest," "the noblest nest / Of warbling SERAPHIM." [109] The
Book of Common Prayer is "A nest of new-born sweets." [110] St.
Teresa's writings are "Nests of new Seraphims here below," and they
hatch the wondering reader's heart into a nest of little eagles and young

---

[106] Martin, p. 279, "To our Blessed Lord upon the Choice of His Sepulcher."
[107] *Ibid.*, p. 100, II, i. *See also* note 96, p. 50.
[108] Crashaw's letter to one of the Ferrar-Collett family, Martin, pp. xxvii-xxxi and
plate, *passim*. For another discussion of this kind of imagery, cf. Joan Bennett, *Four
Metaphysical Poets* (Cambridge, 1953), pp. 100-101.
[109] *Ibid.*, p. 242, l. 119; ll. 105-106. The image occurs also in one of St. Teresa's
poems, IV, "Si el amor que me tenéis," [Peers, III, 283].
[110] Martin, p. 328, l. 2.

loves.[111] The life of Christ is rounded with nests. The shepherds greet the Babe in his "baulmy Nest," and His tomb is a "perfumed Nest." [112] The Lord's bosom is "The bright ambrosiall nest, / Of loue, of life, & euerlasting rest." [113]

The breast is a source of nourishment. In the paraphrase of the Twenty-third Psalm, Crashaw writes: "Plenty weares me at her brest." [114] The connotations of abundance and nurture are obvious. The abundant breast reappears many times: "fruitfull Charities full breasts," "rich Brest," "spatious Bosomes," "bosom fraught with blessings," "Bosom big with Loues," "a swelling bosome," and so on.[115] All holy good flows from "the bosome of the world's best things." [116]

The breasts yield the milk of nourishment. Mary's breasts produce abundantly "Two sister-seas of Virgin-Milk." [117] In the epigrams on the Slaughter of the Innocents the mothers' milk appears often.

> Nor let the milky fonts that bath your thirst,
>   Bee your delay;
> The place that calls you hence, is at the worst
>   Milke all the way.[118]

The epigram turns on the importance of milk in the life of the infant. There is nothing of greater necessity to a nurseling than milk; therefore it is appropriate that the way to heaven is at *worst,* milk all the way (the usual pun).

Similarly, mankind is enjoined "As new-born babes, desire the sincere milk of the word, that ye may grow thereby; If so be that ye have tasted that the Lord is gracious" (I Peter 2.2-3). "O taste and see," the Psalmist sings, "how gracious the Lord is" (34.8); and Crashaw answers, "ten thousand PARADISES / The soul that tasts thee takes from thence." [119] It is then from the Lord, from the nourishing principle of life and salvation, that Crashaw tastes unlimited bliss. This nourishing milk of life from Christ is His blood. It issues from the wound in His side as John had recorded. By suggestion and metonymy the wound in the side is specifically the breast.

---

[111] *Ibid.,* p. 325, l. 46; p. 323, ll. 24-27.
[112] *Ibid.,* p. 249, l. 31, p. 100, II, l. 6.
[113] *Ibid.,* p. 333, ll. 52-53.
[114] *Ibid.,* p. 103, l. 10.
[115] *Ibid.,* p. 139, l. 55; p. 302, l. 8; p. 317, l. 10; p. 329, l. 41; p. 243, l. 160; p. 331, l. 117. *See also* Chap. II, Sec. 1.
[116] *Ibid.,* p. 339, l. 26. The printer's device for the Cambridge University Press shared this emphatic statement of nourishment (p. 5).
[117] *Ibid.,* p. 250, l. 87.
[118] *Ibid.,* p. 88, II.
[119] *Ibid.,* p. 244, ll. 187-188.

> Lo, how the streames of life, [flow] from that full nest
> Of loues, thy lord's too liberall brest.[120]

The image of the nourishing breast of Jesus, a maternal breast actually, is a devotional metaphor found in the Psalms and in even the Protestant poets. Herbert writes, "Show yᵗ thy brests can not be dry,/ . . . . So wee may cease to suck,"[121] and Vaughan, "Wee are thy Infants, and suck thee."[122] St. Teresa reverses the sexes by assigning the breast to the male Christ and the sucking to the Bride.

> But when this most wealthy Spouse desires to enrich and comfort the Bride still more, He draws her so closely to Him that she is like one who swoons from excess of pleasure and joy and seems to be suspended in those Divine arms and drawn near to that sacred side and to those Divine breasts. Sustained by that Divine milk with which her Spouse continually nourishes her and growing in grace so that she may be enabled to receive His comforts, she can do nothing but rejoice.[123]

There can be no shock to find at the end of this succession, Crashaw reducing the image to its final terms, reversing the sexes, and, recognizing that though Christ is Mary's Child He is also her Parent, writing

> Suppose he had been Tabled at thy Teates,
> Thy hunger feeles not what he eates:
> Hee'l have his Teat e're long (a bloody one)
> The Mother then must suck the Son.[124]

6. Hardness and Softness

The contrasts of hardness with softness, coldness with warmth, iciness with thawing apply generally to the human heart in the imagery most often used as the epitome of hardness and coldness, the stone or rock. Crashaw confesses his own "carcasse of a hard, cold, hart."[125] The

---

[120] *Ibid.*, p. 277, II, ii.

[121] Herbert, "Whitsunday," early version in the Williams manuscript [Hutchinson, p. 59].

[122] Vaughan, "Admission" [Martin, p. 453].

[123] St. Teresa, *Conceptions of the Love of God*, IV [Peers, II, 384]. The passage glosses Canticum Canticorum 1.1 and continues to fuse the concepts of nourishment and inebriation ("meliora sunt ubera tua vino"). The idea that one may become drunk on this heavenly milk is not really present in Crashaw unless possibly in "O let me suck the wine . . . Till drunk . . . I be" (Martin, *Crashaw*, p. 287, xi).

[124] Martin, p. 94, II. We have already discussed the parent-child relationship. Miss Tuve remarks (p. 174) that Herbert deleted the image from one of his poems (*see* my note 121): it gives "modern readers troubles whose results I shudder to contemplate." Two such modern readers are Empson (p. 221) and Adams (p. 69).

[125] Martin, p. 326, l. 86.

hearts of men are "the Rocks / Of your owne doubt," "all stone." [126]
Rocks are "relentlesse" and "stubborn," [127] but they are not so hard as
the hearts of men. The stones that the Jews hurl at St. Stephen,

> Ista potest tolerare; potest nescire; sed illi,
> Quæ sunt in vestro pectore, saxa nocent.[128]

At the sixth hour of the day of the Crucifixion, the groans of Christ
"taught attention eu'n to rocks & stones," [129] but not to some hearts:

> there were Rocks would not relent at This.
> Lo, for their own hearts, they rend his.
> Their deadly hate liues still.[130]

But the miracle can happen: hardness can soften; coldness can warm;
iciness can thaw. Christ can "thaw this cold" and make a "melting
heart." [131] When Christ warms and kindles the hard, cold, flinty stone
of man's heart, sparks of the fire of holy love may be struck off. St.
Teresa's books glow with heavenly words "by whose hid flame / Our
hard Hearts shall strike fire." [132]

At the prospect of the Virgin weeping at the foot of the cross, Crashaw speaks to his heart and eyes:

> What kind of marble than
> Is that cold man
> Who can look on & see,
> Nor keep such noble sorrowes company?
> Sure eu'en from you
> (My Flints) some drops are due.[133]

(ii)

---

[126] *Ibid.*, p. 89, ll. 13-14 "Why are yee afraid"; p. 286, vi. The anecdote that Martin
(p. xxxvii) preserves of Crashaw contains certainly a typical image: when Crashaw,
applying to the Pope for "a happy maintenance," received only twenty pistoles, he
remarked that if the Roman church was not founded upon a rock, it was at least founded
upon something as hard as a rock.

[127] *Ibid.*, p. 335, l. 15; p. 245, l. 230.

[128] *Ibid.*, p. 24, I.

[129] *Ibid.*, p. 271, Hymn; the image is lacking in the Latin original. Cf. Matthew
27.51: "and the rocks rent."

[130] *Ibid.*, p. 273, Hymn, "Office of the Holy Cross"; the image is lacking in the Latin
original. The first line recalls the attitude in the preceding quotation; the verse (Matthew
27.51) is in the Gospel for Palm Sunday (Book of Common Prayer, 1549, etc.). The
second line recalls Joel 2.13 and describes the correct way to be repentant, "rend your
heart, and not your garments." This verse is in the Epistle for Ash Wednesday (Book of
Common Prayer, 1549 etc.).

[131] Martin, p. 237, l. 27; p. 320, l. 136. *See also* p. 330, ll. 73-74; p. 308, i.

[132] *Ibid.*, p. 321, ll. 159-160.

[133] *Ibid.*, p. 284-285, "Sancta Maria Dolorum." *See* Psalm 114.8.

And in an image which combines the concept of maternal protection with the hardness and coldness of the sinner, he continues:

> O in that brest
> Of thine (the noblest nest
> Both of loue's fires & flouds) might I recline
> This hard, cold Heart of mine!
> The chill lump would relent, & proue
> Soft subject for the seige of loue.
>
> (v)

The key word in the passage is "relent"; it is the fulcrum on which the whole figure depends. Crashaw uses the word with its meaning "to grow soft," "to liquefy." The chill of the cold heart, lodged in the warm and fiery breast of the Virgin, will grow less frigid and become tractable to the warmth of holy love; the solidness of the hard lump, allowed to float in the nourishingly moist nest of the Virgin, will soften and become a willing and yielding victim for the attacks of the Love God.

7. The Commercial Image

There are two business transactions in the New Testament that are represented in Crashaw's poetry. The first Crashaw refers to only once: it is the sale of Christ by Judas.

> The world's price sett to sale, & by the bold
> Merchants of Death & sin, is bought & sold.[134]

Judas' business dealings do not concern Crashaw further. He is interested in the other, major transaction: it is the purchase of mankind (the redemption of the world) by Christ, "the world's price." At the Last Day Crashaw pleads,

> Iust mercy then, thy Reckning be
> With my price, & not with me
> 'Twas pay'd at first with too much pain,
> To be pay'd twice; or once in vain.[135]

Christ paid for the sins of the world on the cross, and it is in three poems dealing with the Passion that the image is most effectively employed: "The Office of the Holy Cross," "Hymn of the Holy Cross," and "Charitas Nimia." The cross is a scales:

[134] Martin, p. 265, Hymn, "Office of the Holy Cross." The Latin original has only "A Judeis venditus" [Maskell, p. x].

[135] Martin, p. 300, x, "Hymn of the Church in Meditation of the Day of Judgment." The image is not in the original Latin.

> Vs with our price thou weighed'st;
> Our price for vs thou payed'st.[136]

Man's response to Christ's purchase is, naturally, indebtedness:

> Thy life is one long Debt
> Of loue to Him, who on this painfull TREE
> Paid back the flesh he took for thee.[137]

The perversion of the business image adds to its symbolic effectiveness. The Redeemer "greedy of such sad gain / Vsurp't the Portion of THY pain." [138] Christ is anxious to make even the profit that comes from pain; He buys up the shares of the small stockholders and suffers for them in the general depression. This is not good business by earthly criteria, but such poor management is the glory of the Christian religion. Crashaw uses this wonderfully good bad business in "Charitas Nimia."

> Lord, what is man? that thou hast ouerbought
> So much a thing of nought?
> Loue is too kind, I see; & can
> Make but a simple merchant man.[139]

God allows himself to be judged of so little business acumen that He is willing to pay the supreme price for the "sorry merchandise" of mankind.

> O my SAVIOVR, make me see
> How dearly thou hast payd for me
>
> That lost again my LIFE may proue
> As then in DEATH, so now in loue.[140]

"Whosoever will save his life, shall lose it; and whosoever will lose his life for my sake, shall find it" (Matthew 16.25).[141]

Man has his business too. He has "Bargain'd with Death & well-beseeming dust," but he is redeemed by purchase and permitted to "plead shares / In the Æternity of thy old cares." [142] The Magdalene and Christ have business transactions; she pays pearl tears to Him, and He repays in ruby blood. St. Teresa goes off to the Moors to

---

136 *Ibid.*, p. 278, vl, "Hymn of the Holy Cross."
137 *Ibid.*, p. 277, i.
138 *Ibid.*, p. 278, iii.
139 *Ibid.*, p. 280, ll. 3-7.
140 *Ibid.*, p. 282, ll. 63-66.
141 For an epigram on this verse, p. 381, I.
142 *Ibid.*, p. 281, ll. 56, 31-32.

> trade with them,
> For this vnualued Diadem.
> She'l offer them her dearest Breath,
> With CHRIST's Name in't, in change for death.
> Sh'el bargain with them; & will giue
> Them GOD.[143]

Crashaw hastens to "claim shares"[144] with the sorrow of the Virgin and to assume his part of the suffering of Christ.

> Shall I, sett there
> So deep a share
> (Dear Wounds) & onely now
> In sorrows draw no Diuidend with you?[145]

He urges the Countess of Denbigh to hasten into the Roman Church; her delay would seem to indicate that she thought

> the Bargain had been driven
> So hardly betwixt Earth and Heaven;
> Our God would thrive too fast, and be
> Too much a gainer by't, should we
> Our purchas'd selves too soon bestow
> On him.[146]

The commercial image occurs in Crashaw's "Recommendation" of his Hours of the "Office of the Holy Cross." It is the only place in which Crashaw speaks directly to the Deity to offer his poems. It unites the artist and the man, the Poet and the Saint, and is a fitting epitaph to the humble sinner.

> These Houres, & that which houer's o're my E N D,
> Into thy hands, and hart, lord, I commend.

> Take Both to Thine Account, that I & mine
> In that Hour, & in these, may be all thine.[147]

---

[143] *Ibid.*, p. 318, ll. 47-52, "Hymn to St. Teresa." Crashaw has himself cited Chap. I of St. Teresa's autobiography in a marginal note to this passage on a manuscript copy of the "Hymn" (Martin, p. xciii).

[144] *Ibid.*, p. 286, vi.

[145] *Ibid.*, p. 286, ix.

[146] *Ibid.*, p. 349, ll. 61-66, *Letter to the Countess of Denbigh.*

[147] *Ibid.*, p. 276, ll. 1-4.

8. Crashaw's Cosmology

Crashaw implicitly reflects the Ptolemaic universe in his poetry. He expounds the old astronomy with such thoroughness that it is possible to reconstruct many details.[148] At the same time it is impossible to believe that Crashaw was unaware of the new findings, for they were common knowledge, and the advanced thought of the movement had received some of its nurture in Crashaw's father's college, St. John's, Cambridge, through such men as John Cheke, John Dee, and William Gilbert.[149] Crashaw must have regarded himself as unconcerned with any astronomical discoveries and as content to accept the time-honored system of the universe maintained by St. Thomas Aquinas.[150] Such an attitude might seem to catalogue Crashaw as "old-fashioned" in his time, but it would be well to recall that he was in company with many intellectuals, scientific thinkers, and men of prominence. In 1640 appeared a new edition of Sir Francis Bacon's *Advancement of Learning* (in an English translation) and in 1645 Sir Thomas Browne's *Pseudodoxia Epidemica,* both of which attempted to refute the Copernican theory.[151] Such testimony substantiates the hypothesis that though "the scholastic philosophy had been shaken by the new astronomy, . . . it was still largely in control." [152]

At the center of the universe, "where one Center reconciles all things," [153] rolls the Earth, the gathering point of the heaviest things in the universe, which draws to itself all the dross and outscourings of the rest of the creation to become virtually a "Guilded dunghill." Surrounding the Earth is a sphere of water (i.e., the oceans) and around that a sphere of air; the combination of the two elements produces, "in this lower sphear / Of froth & bubbles," only "Oathes of water, words of wind." [154] As change and imperfection are to be expected of matter and of mankind under the Moon, meteors occur and lovers are false.

---

[148] In the "Sospetto d'Herode" occurs the only passage even admitting of a Copernican interpretation: "Looke in what Pompe the Mistresse Planet moves / Rev'rently circled by the lesser seaven" (Martin, p. 117, xxx). Stanza five in the same poem strongly suggests the geocentric universe. The confusion is compounded by reference to the original of Marino, which presumably intended the "Mistresse Planet" to be the moon: "Che come suol la Candida facella / Scintillar frà le lampadi minori." T. R. translates: "Which as the Moon; when lesser stars appear, / Above their luster, doth her rayes improve." It may be that the lesser seven are the Pleiades.

[149] Francis R. Johnson, *Astronomical Thought in Renaissance England* (Baltimore, 1937), pp. 215-216.

[150] *Summa,* Pt. I, Q. lxviii, Art. 4.

[151] Johnson, p. 335; *Pseudodoxia Epidemica,* VI, 5; Basil Willey, *The Seventeenth-Century Background* (New York, 1950), *passim.*

[152] William P. Dunn, *Sir Thomas Browne* (Minneapolis, 1950), p. 11.

[153] Martin, p. 110, v; *see* Praz, p. 233.

[154] Martin, p. 332, ll. 14, 8-9, 17.

Though the Earth is corrupt, it looks upward to better things. Crashaw carries his readers exultingly through the seven concentric spheres of the planets, passing by the "circling Sun," while the orbs maintain "their faithful rounds," until he comes to the eighth sphere, the sphere of the constellations, the Milky Way, and the fixed stars — the Firmament, in short, that incloses the "self inuoluing Sett of Sphears."[155] On such a voyage the Virgin Mary is assumed on her way to her heavenly home. She is

> Purer & brighter
> Then the chast starres, whose choise lamps come to light her
> While through the crystall orbes, clearer then they
> She climbes; and makes a farre more milkey way.[156]

The fixed stars in the eighth sphere[157] were associated by the scholastics with the souls of the blessed departed. Crashaw speaks of a soul newly released from the bonds of mortality as taking "vp among the starres a room" where it will fill "a bright place, / Mongst those immortall fires" and "take acquaintance of the spheare, / And all the smooth faced kindred there."[158] In his desire to encourage the Countess of Denbigh to embrace the Roman Catholic Church, Crashaw uses the concepts of permanence and residence poetically, praying that Christ "fix this fair INDEFINITE . . . And of a meteor make a starr."[159] The image is utilized again in a similar sense when he recommends the virtues and advantages of the life of religious contemplation as practiced at Little Gidding:

> The self-remembring SOVL sweetly recouers
> Her kindred with the starrs; not basely houers
> Below: But meditates her immortall way
> Home to the originall sourse of LIGHT & intellectuall
>   Day.[160]

The seven spheres of the planets and the eighth sphere of the fixed stars constitute The First Heavens. Enveloping The First Heavens is the ninth sphere, or The Second Heavens. This is the sphere of the circumambient waters "that be above the firmament"; it is "acqueous or crystalline, wholly transparent."[161] The characteristics of these waters

---

[155] *Ibid.*, p. 299, iii; p. 280, l. 18; p. 240, l. 30. The "Sett" is in a container, the "huge Chest / Of Heauns."

[156] *Ibid.*, p. 304, ll. 3-6, "Assumption."

[157] These stars will remain fixed until the Last Day "When starres themselues shall stagger" (*ibid.*, p. 300, vi).

[158] *Ibid.*, p. 310, xii; p. 164, ll. 9-10; p. 130, ll. 13-14.

[159] *Ibid.*, p. 237, ll. 31, 30.

[160] *Ibid.*, p. 339, ll. 37-39, "Description of a Religious House."

[161] *Summa*, Pt. I, Q. lxviii, Art. 2.

baffled Crashaw as they had previously baffled St. Thomas and others
before him. But in the tears of "The Weeper" Crashaw succeeds in
identifying them:

> Waters aboue th'Heauns, what they be
> We'are taught best by thy Teares & thee.[162]

The tenth sphere, surrounding the sphere of the heavenly waters,
forms The Third Heavens, and appears to be the primary residence of
God. It is composed of light, and for that reason is named the Empyrean.
It is to this sphere that St. Paul was rapt in his mystical vision (2
Corinthians 12.2-4): "I knew a man in Christ above fourteen years
ago . . . such an one caught up to the third heaven. . . . How that he
was caught up into paradise and heard unspeakable words." The words
heard by St. Paul, Crashaw reports in the "Hymn to the Name above
every Name, the Name of Jesus," are a hymn of praise to the name
of Jesus. It is the privilege of mankind in a small and imperfect way
to join in this paean of praise: "We . . . haue leaue to doe/ The Same
bright Busynes (ye Third Heavens) with you."[163] Within The Third
Heavens stands the throne of the Almighty with Christ sitting on the
right hand. Hence he descended to Earth to redeem mankind and is
ever ready to return again when called for.

> Nor can the cares of his whole Crown
> (When one poor Sigh sends for him down)
> Detain him, but he leaves behind
> The late wings of the lazy Wind,
> Spurns the tame Laws of Time and Place,
> And breaks through all ten Heav'ns to our embrace.[164]

Farther than The Third Heavens it is impossible to proceed; space is
curved:

> Heavens have no bound,
> But in their infinite and endless Round
> Embrace themselves.[165]

The spheres of the Ptolemaic system by virtue of their beauty, purity,
perfection, and completeness serve Crashaw as symbols of Christ. Crashaw intimates that there is no "fairer Spheare" than Christ, and he
adds that the whole world is insufficient to make up Christ's "half-

---

162 Martin, p. 309, iv.
163 *Ibid.*, p. 242, ll. 109-110.
164 *Ibid.*, pp. 349-350, ll. 73-78, *Letter to the Countess of Denbigh.*
165 *Ibid.*, p. 178, after l. 65, 1648 version.

sphear."[166] The scholastic concept devised by Hermes Trismegistus of God as a "circle, whose center is everywhere, and whose circumference nowhere" was adopted by Sir Thomas Browne [167] and paraphrased by Crashaw as "All-circling point. All centring sphear."[168]

According to scholastic philosophy, the spinning of the orbs concentrically produced the music of the spheres. For Crashaw too "the singing Orbes" are attuned and form as it were "A set of rarest harmony."[169] Man in his fallen state is too sinful to hear these celestial harmonies;

> Nor was't our deafnes, but our sins, that thus
> Long made th'Harmonious orbes all mute to vs.[170]

Were man unfallen, these harmonies might still ravish his soul by the beauty of their music and lift it

> through all the sphæares
> Of Musicks heaven; and seat it there on high
> In th' *Empyræum* of pure Harmony.[171]

Though Man cannot hear the music of the spheres, he has yet the opportunity of joining in this empyrean harmony. Since "All Things that Are, / Or, what's the same, / Are Musicall"[172] share in the creation, so they may share in this celestial harmony. "We in thy prayse will haue our parts," says Crashaw, "Our Murmurs haue their Musick too, / Ye mighty ORBES, as well as you."[173] But though man must play on "so farr inferior LYRES," he may be so fortunate that Heaven will reach down "Harpes of heaun to hands of man".[174] Crashaw encourages mankind:

> Thou too hast thy Part
> And Place in the Great Throng
> Of this vnbounded All-imbracing SONG.[175]

The epicyclic revolutions of the spheres were considered also as a universal dance. "The joyfull sphæres with a delicious sound / . . . dance a round / To their owne Musick."[176] The movement of the

---

[166] *Ibid.*, p. 89, I; p. 255, 1. 41
[167] Dunn, pp. 43, 54.
[168] Martin, p. 255, 1. 26. *See also* the quotation from Dionysius' Letters in Chap. II.
[169] *Ibid.*, p. 85, vii; p. 343, 1. 36.
[170] *Ibid.*, p. 257, ll. 132-133, "Epiphany Hymn."
[171] *Ibid.*, p. 153, ll. 148-150, "Musicks Duel."
[172] *Ibid.*, p. 241, ll. 56-58.
[173] *Ibid.*, p. 305, 1. 45; p. 242, ll. 103-104.
[174] *Ibid.*, p. 242, 1. 102; p. 294, i.
[175] *Ibid.*, p. 241, ll. 89-91, "Hymn to the Name of Jesus."
[176] *Ibid.*, p. 390, ll. 21-23.

orbes, since it is in tune with the music of the empyrean — "lett heauens quire / Ravish the dancing orbes" — is a "Golden Dance," "a joyfull round," and at the Latter Day "circular joyes / [Shall] Dance in an endlesse round." [177]

The astronomical bodies exert influence on the lives of earth dwellers. In a secular poem, Venus, attempting to discover Cupid's horoscope,

> consults the conscious Spheares,
> To calculate her young sons yeares.
> Shee askes if sad, or saving powers,
> Gave Omen to his infant howers,
> Shee asks each starre that then stood by,
> If poore Love shall live or dy. [178]

The influence of the stars is employed to hyperbolize the royal children who "Fixt in your sphæres of glory" are urged to "shed from thence / The treasures of our liues, your influence." [179] Hope defies the "conspiring starres," but a bereaved wife laments, "Sure in my early woes starres were at strife." [180] The image has a much richer significance in the religious poems. The dart of mystical love, dipped thrice in the flame of love, writes the name of Jesus

> Vpon the roof of Heau'n; where ay
> It shines, & with a soueraign ray
> Beates bright vpon the burning faces
> Of soules which in that name's sweet graces
> Find euerlasting smiles. [181]

These references to the Ptolemaic system of the universe call attention to three considerations in Crashaw's poetry and life. It appears first by the frequency of the references to the Ptolemaic system and by the fact that they disclose no doubts that Crashaw believed faithfully and completely in this traditional system. His reasons for this support of the system — if indeed he ever paused to consider as support his acceptance of what he must have regarded as a commonplace — were surely logical as well as theological. A second consideration, one no less important to the poet, was the fact that the system had acquired by the seventeenth century a wealth of poetic connotation and convention, so that it appeared as readily as a figure of speech as it did a description of the uni-

---

[177] *Ibid.*, p. 389, ll. 1-2; p. 116, xxvi; p. 391, l. 32; p. 168, ll. 37-38. The image of the golden dance Crashaw has contributed to his Italian original, the "Sospetto d'Herode."
[178] *Ibid.*, p. 185, II, i, "Loves Horoscope."
[179] *Ibid.*, p. 390, ll. 39-40.
[180] *Ibid.*, p. 346, l. 32; p. 334, l. 5.
[181] *Ibid.*, p. 319, ll. 83-87, "Hymn to St. Teresa."

verse. The poetic conventions which appealed to most of the poets of the century were both religious and secular; it should therefore be no surprise to find the system carefully represented in image and metaphor in Crashaw's sacred and profane poetry. Finally, the most important consideration stems from a combination of the other two. The Ptolemaic system was most useful to the Christian poet because it could be utilized for Christian purposes. Thanks to the missionary zeal of the scholastics, the Ptolemaic system had become Christianized, and the pagan spheres bespoke now a well-ordered universe and a wise and provident God. The system materialized a clearly defined will of the creating God, it was useful symbolically to depict the perfection of divinity, and it could be accommodated to a metaphor of the Christian life in this world as in the next.

BIBLIOGRAPHY

1. Texts

Analecta hymnica medii aevi, ed. Guido Maria Dreves, *et al.*, Leipzig: R. Reisland, 1886-1922.

Andrewes, Lancelot, *Ninety-six Sermons*. Oxford: John Parker, 1841.

Aquinas, Saint Thomas, *The Basic Writings of Saint Thomas Aquinas*, ed. Anton C. Pegis. New York: Random House, 1945.

————, *The Summa Contra Gentiles*, trans. by The English Dominican Fathers from the Latest Leonine Edit., 4 vols. London: Burns Oates & Washbourne Ltd., 1928.

————, *Summa Theologica*, tr. by The Fathers of the English Dominican Province, 2nd edit., 22 vols. London: Burns Oates & Washbourne Ltd., 1920-1922.

————, *Summa Theologica*, ed. Card. Joseph Pecci, 4th edit., 4 vols. Paris: P. Lethielleux, [1927].

————, *Summa Theologica*, ed. Institute of Medieval Studies of Ottawa, 4 vols. Ottawa: Dominican College of Ottawa, 1941.

Holy Bible, The King James Version. New York: Oxford University Press, n.d.

————, trans. from The Latin Vulgate (Douai Edit.). New York: D. & J. Sadlier, [1845].

————, Vulgatae Editionis, Sixti V. et Clementis VIII. London: Samuel Bagster and Sons, [1827].

————, *The Apocrypha*, according to the Authorized Version. Oxford: The Clarendon Press, n.d.

Browne, Sir Thomas, *The Works of Sir Thomas Browne*, ed. Geoffrey Keynes, 6 vols. London: Faber & Gwyer, 1928.

Catena Aurea, 4 vols. Oxford: John Parker, 1841.

Cowley, Abraham, *Poems*, ed. A. R. Waller. Cambridge: The University Press, 1905.

Crashaw, Richard, *Epigrammata Sacra Selecta, cum Anglica Versione. Sacred Epigrams Englished*. [trans. Clement Barksdale] London: John Barksdale, 1682.

————, *The Complete Works of Richard Crashaw*, ed. Alexander B. Grosart, 2 vols. Fuller Worthies' Library, 1873.

————, *Steps to the Temple Delights of the Muses and Other Poems*, ed. A. R. Waller. Cambridge: The University Press, 1904.

————, "A Hitherto Unpublished Poem by (?) Richard Crashaw," ed. L. C. Martin, *London Mercury*, VIII (May 1923), 159-166.

————, *The Poems English Latin and Greek of Richard Crashaw*, ed. L. C. Martin. Oxford: The Clarendon Press, 1927. 2nd edit., revised, 1957.

———, "An Overlooked Poem by Richard Crashaw," suggested by B. H. Newdigate, *London Mercury* XXXII (July 1935), 265-266.

Dionysius the Areopagite, *The Works of Dionysius the Areopagite*, trans. John Parker, 2 vols. in one. London: James Parker & Co., 1897.

The First Prayer-Book of Edward VI. Compared with the Successive Revisions of the Book of Common Prayer. Oxford and London: John Parker, 1877.

Fletcher, Giles, and Fletcher, Phineas, *Poetical Works*, ed. Frederick S. Boas, 2 vols. Cambridge: The University Press, 1909.

Grotius, Hugo, *Poemata Collecta* . . . Lugdun. Batav. 1637.

———, *Christ's Passion*, trans. George Sandys, 2nd edit. London: T. Bassett, 1687.

Haeftenus, D. Benedictus, *Regia via crucis*. Antverpiae: Vltraiectino, 1635.

Herbert, George, *The Temple. Sacred Poems, and Private Ejaculations*, 12th edit. London: Jeffery Wale, 1703.

———, *The English Works of George Herbert. Newly Arranged and Annotated and Considered in Relation to His Life*, by George Herbert Palmer, 3 vols. Boston and New York: Houghton Mifflin and Co., MDCCCCV.

———, *The Works of George Herbert*, ed. with a Commentary by F. E. Hutchinson. Oxford: The Clarendon Press, 1941.

Hooker, Richard, *The Works of that Learned and Judicious Divine, Mr. Richard Hooker.* 2 vols. Oxford: University Press, MDCCCL.

St. John of the Cross, *The Complete Works of Saint John of the Cross*, trans. and ed. by E. Allison Peers, 3 vols., rev. edit. London: Burns Oates & Washbourne, 1953.

Justa Edovardo King naufrago, ab Amicis moerentibus. Cambridge: The University Press, 1638. [Publication #45, The Facsimile Text Society. New York: Columbia University Press, 1939].

Marino, Giambattista, *Strage de gli Innocenti* . . . Venetia: Presso Giacomo Scaglia, MDCXXXIII.

———, *The Slaughter of the Innocents* . . . By the famous Poet the Cavalier Marino. Trans. by T. A. London: Samuel Mearne, 1675.

Maskell, William, *Monumenta Ritualia Ecclesiae Anglicanae*, 3 vols., 2nd edit. Oxford: The Clarendon Press, 1882.

Migne, Jacques Paul, ed., *Patrologiae cursus completus* . . . *Series Latina*, 221 vols. Parisiis: Migne, 1844-1865.

Milton, John, *The Student's Milton. Being the complete poems of John Milton*, ed. Frank Allen Patterson, rev. edit. New York: F. S. Crofts & Co., 1947.

Mone, F. J., *Hymni Latini Medii Aevi*. Freiburg: Herder, 1853.

Morris, Richard, *Legends of the Holy Rood; Symbols of the Passion and Cross-Poems.* London: E.E.T.S. #46, 1871.

Plutarch, *Moralia: Isis and Osiris*, ed. and trans. by Frank C. Babbitt [*Loeb Classical Library*]. London: Heinemann, 1936.

Aurelius Prudentius Clemens, *Works*, ed. and trans. by H. J. Thomson [*Loeb Classical Library*]. London: Hienemann, 1949.

The Roman Missal in Latin and English, ed. Abbot Cabrol. New York: P. J. Kennedy & Sons, 1930.

Southwell, Robert, *The Complete Poems* . . ., ed. Alexander B. Grosart. Fuller Worthies' Library, 1872.

————, *A Foure-Fold Meditation of the foure last things.* [*The Isham Reprints* #4]. London: Elkin Mathews, MDCCCXCV.

————, *Marie Magdalen's Funerall Teares* . . . London: Charles Baldwyn, 1823.

St. Teresa of Jesus, *The Complete Works of Saint Teresa of Jesus,* trans. and ed. E. Allison Peers from the critical edit. of P. Silverio de Santa Teresa, 3 vols. London: Sheed & Ward, 1946.

————, *The Flaming Hart or the Life of the Glorious S. Teresa.* Antwerp: Johannes Meursius, 1642.

————, *The Life of Saint Teresa of Avila by Herself,* trans. J. M. Cohen. Harmondsworth: Penguin Books, 1957.

————, *Escritos de Santa Teresa,* ed. Don Vicente de la Fuente, 2 vols. [*Biblioteca de Autores Españoles,* vols. 53 and 55]. Madrid: M. Rivadeneyra, 1877.

Vaughan, Henry, *The Works of Henry Vaughan,* ed. L. C. Martin. Oxford: The Clarendon Press, 1957.

2. General Works

Anon., "Poet and Saint," (London) *Times Literary Supplement,* 1 June 1946, p. 258.

Anon., "A Poet of Delights," (London) *Times Literary Supplement,* 19 August 1949.

Adams, Robert Martin, "Taste and Bad Taste in Metaphysical Poetry," *Hudson Review,* VIII (Spring 1955), 61-77.

Allen, Don Cameron, "Symbolic Color in the Literature of the English Renaissance," *PQ,* XV (January 1936), 81-90.

Allison, Antony F., "Crashaw and St. François de Sales," *RES,* XXIV (October 1948), 295-302.

————, "Some Influences in Crashaw's Poem 'On a Prayer Booke sent to Mrs. M. R.,'" *RES,* XXIII (January 1947), 34-42.

Alvarez, A., *The School of Donne.* London: Chatto and Windus, 1961.

Barker, Arthur, "The Pattern of Milton's *Nativity Ode,*" *University of Toronto Quarterly,* X (January 1941), 167-181.

Barker, Francis E., "Crashaw and Andrewes," (London) *Times Literary Supplement,* 21 August 1937, p. 608.

————, "The Religious Poetry of Richard Crashaw," *Church Quarterly Review,* XCVI (April 1923), 39-65.

Beachcroft, T. O., "Crashaw—and the Baroque Style," *Criterion,* XIII (April 1934), 407-425.

Beeching, Canon [H. C.], Introduction to *The Poems of Richard Crashaw,* ed. J. R. Tutin. London: George Routledge & Sons, 1905.

Bennett, Joan, *Four Metaphysical Poets* ["Richard Crashaw"]. Cambridge: The University Press, 1934.

Blackstone, B[ernard], ed., *The Ferrar Papers.* Cambridge: The University Press, 1938.

Bottrall, Margaret, *George Herbert.* London: John Murray, 1954.

Bradner, Leicester, *Musae Anglicanae.* New York: Modern Language Assn., 1940.

Buffum, Imbrie, *Agrippa d'Aubigné's* Les Tragiques: *A Study of the Baroque Style in Poetry* [*Yale Romanic Studies*: Second Series, No. 1]. New Haven: Yale University Press, 1951.

———, *Studies in the Baroque from Montaigne to Rotrou* [*Yale Romanic Studies*: Second Series, No. 4]. New Haven: Yale University Press, 1957.

Bush, Douglas, *English Literature in the Earlier Seventeenth Century* 1600-1660 [*The Oxford History of English Literature*, vol. V]. Oxford: The Clarendon Press, 1946.

(Lord) Chalmers, "Richard Crashaw: Poet and Saint," *In Memoriam Adolphus William Ward, Master of Peterhouse.* Cambridge: The University Press, 1924.

Collmer, Robert G., "Crashaw's 'Death more misticall and high,' " *JEGP*, LV (July 1956), 373-380.

Colville, K. N., "Crashaw and Andrewes," (London) *Times Literary Supplement*, 28 August 1937, p. 624.

Confrey, Burton, "A Note on Richard Crashaw," *MLN*, XXXVII (April 1922), 250-251.

Cook, Albert S., "Notes on Milton's *Ode on the Morning of Christ's Nativity*," *Transactions of the Connecticut Academy of Arts and Sciences*, XV (1909), 305-368.

Dillistone, F. W., *Christianity and Symbolism.* London: Collins, 1955.

Dunbar, H. Flanders, *Symbolism in Medieval Thought.* New Haven: Yale University Press, 1929.

Dunn, William P., *Sir Thomas Browne.* Minneapolis: University of Minnesota Press, 1950.

Eliot, T. S., *For Lancelot Andrewes* ["A Note on Richard Crashaw" (A Review of L. C. Martin's Edition)]. London: Faber and Gwyer, 1928.

Empson, William, *Seven Types of Ambiguity.* London: Chatto and Windus, 1956.

Esch, Arno, *Englische Religiöse Lyrik des 17. Jahrhunderts . . .* Tübingen: Max Niemeyer, 1955.

Ewer, Mary Anita, *A Survey of Mystical Symbolism.* London: S.P.C.K., 1933.

Falls, Cyril, "The Divine Poet," *The Nineteenth Century*, XCIII (February 1923), 225-232.

Farnham, Anthony E., "St. Teresa and the Coy Mistress," *Boston University Studies in English*, II (Winter 1956), 226-239.

Freeman, Rosemary, *English Emblem Books.* London: Chatto & Windus, 1948.

Garth, Helen Meredith, *Saint Mary Magdalene in Medieval Literature.* Baltimore: The Johns Hopkins Press, 1950.

Gosse, Sir Edmund W., *Seventeenth-Century Studies* ["Richard Crashaw"], 2nd edit. London: Kegan Paul, Trench & Co., 1885.

Green, E. Tyrrell, *The Thirty-nine Articles and the Age of the Reformation An Historical and Doctrinal Exposition in the Light of Contemporary Documents.* London: Wells, Gardner, Darton & Co., 1896.

Greenlaw, Edwin, Review of L. C. Martin, *The Poems . . . of Richard Crashaw*, *MLN*, XLIII (April 1928), 275-278.

Gummere, F. B., "On the Symbolic Use of the Colors Black and White in Germanic Tradition," *Haverford College Studies*, I (1889), 112-162.

Heninger, S. K., Jr., *A Handbook of Renaissance Meteorology.* Durham, N. C.: Duke University Press, 1960.

Holliday, Carl, *The Cavalier Poets Their Lives, Their Day, and Their Poetry* ["Richard Crashaw"]. New York and Washington: Neale Publishing Co., 1911.

Holmes, Elizabeth, *Aspects of Elizabethan Imagery*. Oxford: Blackwell, 1929.

Horne, David H., *The Life and Minor Works of George Peele*. New Haven: Yale University Press, 1952.

Hughes, Merritt Y., "Spenser's Acrasia and the Circe of the Renaissance," *Journal of the History of Ideas*, IV (October 1943), 381-399.

Husain, Itrat, *The Mystical Element in the Metaphysical Poets* . . . Edinburgh: Oliver and Boyd, 1948.

Inge, William Ralph, *Christian Mysticism* [*The Bampton Lectures*, 1899]. New York: Charles Scribner's Sons, 1899.

Janelle, Pierre, *Robert Southwell the Writer*. London: Sheed and Ward, 1935.

Johnson, Francis R., *Astronomical Thought in Renaissance England*. Baltimore: Johns Hopkins Press, 1937.

Lea, Kathleen M., "Conceits," *MLR*, XX (October 1925), 389-406.

Levin, Harry, *The Power of Blackness*. New York: A. A. Knopf, 1958.

Lovejoy, Arthur O., *The Great Chain of Being*. Cambridge: Harvard University Press, 1948.

McCann, Eleanor M., *The Influence of Sixteenth and Seventeenth Century Spanish Mystics and Ascetics on Some Metaphysical Writers*. Unpublished Dissertation, Stanford University, 1953.

Madsden, William G., "A Reading of 'Musicks Duell,'" in *Studies in Honor of John Wilcox*. Detroit: Wayne State University Press, 1958.

Major, H. D. A., Manson, T. W., and Wright, C. J., *The Mission and Message of Jesus An Exposition of the Gospels in the Light of Modern Research*. New York: E. P. Dutton and Co., 1938.

Manning, Stephen, "The Meaning of 'The Weeper,'" *ELH*, XXII (March 1955), 34-47.

Martin, L. C., "An Unedited Crashaw Manuscript," (London) *Times Literary Supplement*, 18 April 1952, p. 272.

Martz, Louis L., *The Poetry of Meditation*. New Haven: Yale University Press, 1954.

Maxwell, J. C., "Steps to the Temple: 1646 and 1648," *PQ*, XXIX (April 1950), 216-220.

Mazzeo, Joseph Anthony, "A Critique of Some Modern Theories of Metaphysical Poetry," *MP*, L (November 1952), 88-96.

Mazzinelli, Abbé Alexander, *The Office of Holy Week*, trans. anon. Baltimore: Kelly, Piet & Co., 1870.

Miles, Josephine, *The Primary Language of Poetry in the 1640's* [*University of California Publications in English*, vol. 19, No. 1, pp. 1-160]. Berkeley and Los Angeles: University of California Press, 1948.

Mitchell, Charles Bradford, *The Translations and Secular Lyrics of Richard Crashaw*, Unpublished Master's Thesis Wesleyan University, Middleton, Conn., 1929.

Moloney, Michael F., "Richard Crashaw," *Catholic World*, CLXII (October 1945), 43-50.

———, "Richard Crashaw," *Catholic World*, CLXIX (August 1949), 336-340.

Monneret de Villard, Ugo, *Le Leggende Orientali sul Magi Evangelici* [*Studi e Testi*, No. 163]. Citta del Vaticano: Biblioteca Apostolica Vaticana, 1952.

de Mourgues, Odette, *Metaphysical Baroque and Précieux Poetry*. Oxford: Clarendon Press, 1953.

Neill, Kerby, "Structure and Symbol in Crashaw's *Hymn in the Nativity*," *PMLA*, LXIII (March 1948), 101-113.

Nelson, Lowry, Jr., *Baroque Lyric Poetry*. New Haven: Yale University Press, 1961.

Nethercot, Arthur H., *Abraham Cowley The Muse's Hannibal*. London: Oxford University Press, MCMXXXI.

Nicolson, Marjorie, "The 'New Astronomy' and English Literary Imagination," *SP*, XXXII (July 1935), 428-462.

Osmond, Percy H., *The Mystical Poets of the English Church*. New York: S.P.C.K., 1919.

Peers, E. Allison, *Spanish Mysticism*. London: Methuen, 1924.

————, *Studies of the Spanish Mystics*, 2 vols. London: Sheldon Press, 1927-1930.

Peter, John, "Crashaw and 'The Weeper,'" *Scrutiny*, XIX (October 1953), 258-273.

Pettoello, Laura, "A Current Misconception concerning the Influence of Marino's Poetry on Crashaw's," *MLR*, LII (July 1957), 321-328.

Powers, Perry J., "Lope de Vega and *Las Lágrimas de la Madalena*," *Comparative Literature*, VIII (Fall 1956), 273-290.

Praz, Mario, *The Flaming Heart: Essays on Crashaw, Machiavelli, and Other Studies in the Relations between Italian and English Literature from Chaucer to T. S. Eliot*. Garden City: Doubleday (Anchor), 1958.

————, *Richard Crashaw*. Brescia: Morcelliana, 1945.

————, "A Source for an Epigram of Crashaw," (London) *Times Literary Supplement*, 21 October 1949, p. 681.

————, *Studies in Seventeenth Century Imagery*, 2 vols., [*Studies of the Warburg Institute*, vol. 3]. London: The Warburg Institute, University of London, 1939-1947.

Price, Hereward T., "Function of Imagery in *Venus and Adonis*," *Papers of the Michigan Academy of Science Arts and Letters*, XXXI (1945), 275-297.

Procter, Francis, *A History of the Book of Common Prayer with A Rationale of its Offices*, 6th edit. London and Cambridge: Macmillan and Co., 1864.

Quiller-Couch, Sir Arthur, *Studies in Literature* ["Traherne, Crashaw and Others"]. New York: G. P. Putnam's Sons, 1918.

Rickey, Mary Ellen, "Chapman and Crashaw," *N&Q*, CCI (November 1956), 472-473.

————, "Crashaw and Vaughan," *N&Q*, CC (June 1955), 232-233.

————, *Rhyme and Meaning in Richard Crashaw*. [Lexington:] University of Kentucky Press, 1961.

Ross, Malcolm Mackenzie, *Poetry and Dogma*. New Brunswick, N. J.: Rutgers University Press, 1954.

Sackville-West, V., *The Eagle and the Dove A Study in Contrasts* ["St. Teresa of Avila"]. London: Michael Joseph Ltd., 1943.

Schroeder, H. J., *Canons and Decrees of the Council of Trent*. St. Louis, Mo., and London: Herder Book Co., 1955.

Sharp, Robert Lathrop, *From Donne to Dryden, The Revolt Against Metaphysical Poetry.* Chapel Hill: University of North Carolina Press, 1940.

Shepherd, R. A. Eric, ed. with an Introductory Study, *The Religious Poems of Richard Crashaw.* London: Manresa Press, 1914.

Siegel, Ben, "Elements of the Old Testament in Early Seventeenth Century English Poetry," pp. 97-99 in *Abstracts of Dissertations, University of Southern California.* Los Angeles, 1957.

Simmons, T. F., ed., *Lay Folks Mass Book.* London: E.E.T.S. #71, 1879.

Sister Miriam Bernard, "More Than a Woman," *Catholic World,* CLX (October 1944), 52-57.

Skard, Sigmund, "The Use of Color in Literature," *Proceedings of the American Philosophical Society,* XC, No. 3 (July 1946), pp. 163-249.

Skipton, H. P. K., *The Life and Times of Nicholas Ferrar.* London: Mowbray & Co., 1907.

Spender, Constance, "Richard Crashaw, 1613-1648," *Contemporary Review,* CXVI (August 1919), 210-215.

Stimson, Dorothy, *The Gradual Acceptance of the Copernican Theory of the Universe.* New York: Baker & Taylor, 1917.

Summers, Joseph H., *George Herbert His Religion and Art.* Cambridge: Harvard University Press, 1954.

Symons, Arthur, "The Poetry of Santa Teresa and San Juan de la Cruz," *Contemporary Review,* LXXV (April 1899), 542-551.

Sypher, Wylie, *Four Stages of Renaissance Style.* Garden City, N. Y.: Doubleday (Anchor), 1955.

Turnell, Martin, "Richard Crashaw after 300 Years," *Nineteenth Century,* CXLVI (August 1949), 100-114.

Tuve, Rosemond, *Elizabethan and Metaphysical Imagery.* Chicago: University of Chicago, 1947.

————, *Images and Themes in Five Poems by Milton.* Cambridge: Harvard University Press, 1957.

————, *A Reading of George Herbert.* Chicago: University of Chicago, 1952.

Wallerstein, Ruth, *Richard Crashaw A Study in Style and Poetic Development* [*University of Wisconsin Studies in Language and Literature,* No. 37]. Madison: University of Wisconsin Press, 1935.

————, *Studies in Seventeenth-Century Poetic.* [Madison]: University of Wisconsin Press, 1950.

Wallis, P. J., "The Library of William Crashawe," *Transactions of the Cambridge Bibliographical Society,* II (1954-1958), 213-228.

Warren, Austin, "Crashaw and St. Teresa," (London) *Times Literary Supplement,* 25 August 1932, p. 593.

————, "Crashaw's 'Apologie,'" (London) *Times Literary Supplement,* 16 November 1935, p. 746.

————, "Crashaw's Epigrammata Sacra," *JEGP,* XXXIII (April 1934), 233-239.

————, "Crashaw's Paintings at Cambridge," *MLN,* XLVIII (1933), 365-366.

————, "Crashaw's Reputation in the Nineteenth Century," *PMLA,* LI (September 1936), 769-785.

————, "Crashaw's Residence at Peterhouse," (London) *Times Literary Supplement,* 3 November 1932, p. 815.

———, "The Mysticism of Richard Crashaw," *Symposium*, IV (1933), 133-155.

———, "The Reputation of Crashaw in the Seventeenth and Eighteenth Centuries," *SP*, XXXI (July 1934), 385-407.

———, "Richard Crashaw, 'Catechist and Curate,'" *MP*, XXXII (February 1935), 261-269.

———, *Richard Crashaw A Study in Baroque Sensibility*. University (La.): Louisiana State University Press, 1939.

Watkin, E. I., "Richard Crashaw," in *The English Way: Studies in English Sanctity*, ed. Maisie Ward (Sheed). London: Sheed & Ward, 1933.

Wells, Henry W., *Poetic Imagery*. New York: Columbia University Press, 1924.

White, Helen C., *The Metaphysical Poets A Study in Religious Experience*. New York: The Macmillan Co., 1936.

White, T. H., *The Book of Beasts*. London: Jonathan Cape, 1954.

Whitehead, Alfred North, *Symbolism Its Meaning and Effect* [*Barbour-Page Lectures*, University of Virginia, 1927] Cambridge: The University Press, 1928.

Willey, Basil, *The Seventeenth Century Background Studies in the Thought of the Age in Relation to Poetry and Religion*. London: Chatto & Windus, 1942.

Williams, George W. "Crashaw's 'Letter to the Countess of Denbigh,'" *Explicator*, VI (1948), No. 7, #48.

———, "Richard Crashaw and the Little Gidding Bookbinders," *N&Q*, CCI (January 1956), 9-10.

———, "Textual Revision in Crashaw's 'Vpon the Bleeding Crucifix,'" *Papers of the Bibliographical Society of the University of Virginia*, I (1948), 191-193.

Williamson, George, *The Donne Tradition A Study in English Poetry from Donne to the Death of Cowley*. Cambridge: Harvard University Press, 1930.

Wilson, Edmund, *Axel's Castle A Study in the Imaginative Literature of 1870-1930* [Ch. I "Symbolism."] New York: Charles Scribner's Sons, 1931.

Wilson, Edward M., "Spanish and English Religious Poetry of the Seventeenth Century," *Journal of Ecclesiastical History*, IX (April 1958), 30-53.

Winters, Yvor, *In Defense of Reason*. New York: Swallow Press & Wm. Morrow and Co., 1947.

Yeats, William B., *Essays* ["The Symbolism of Poetry"]. New York: The Macmillan Co., 1924.

Young, Charles A., *A Text-Book of General Astronomy*, rev. edit. Boston: Ginn & Co., 1904.

3. References

Cruden, Alexander, *A Complete Concordance to the Holy Scriptures . . . to which is added A Concordance to the Books Called Apocrypha*, 4th rev. edit. New York: Dodd, Mead, & Co., 1879.

Delitzsch, F. F., *Biblical Commentary on the Prophecies of Isaiah*, tr. Jas. Denney, 2 vols. New York: Funk & Wagnalls, 1892.

Dutripon, E. P., *Concordantiae Bibliorum Sacrorum Vulgatae Editionis*. Paris: Belin-Mandar, M.DCCC.XXXVIII.

Eiselen, Frederick C., *et al.*, ed., *The Abingdon Bible Commentary*. Nashville: The Abingdon Press, 1929.

Frazer, Sir James George, *The Golden Bough A Study in Magic and Religion*, 12 vols. New York: The Macmillan Co., 1935.

Fry, Edward Alexander, *Almanacks for Students of English History*. London: Phillimore & Co., 1915.

Gilbert, Allan H., *A Geographical Dictionary of Milton* [*Cornell Studies in English*, IV]. New Haven: Yale University Press, MDCCCCXIX.

Hastings, James, *et al.*, ed., *A Dictionary of the Bible Dealing with its Language, Literature, and Contents Including the Biblical Theology*, 5 vols. New York: Charles Scribner's Sons, 1911.

————, *Encyclopaedia of Religion and Ethics*, 13 vols. New York: Charles Scribner's Sons, 1908.

Herberman, Charles G., *et al.*, ed., *The Catholic Encyclopedia An International Work of Reference on the Constitution, Doctrine, Discipline, and History of The Catholic Church*, 15 vols. New York: Robert Appleton Co., 1907.

Plomer, H. R., Bushnell, G. H., and Dix, E. R. McC., *A Dictionary of the Printers and Booksellers who were at work in England, Scotland and Ireland from 1726 to 1775* [The Bibliographical Society (Oxford)]. Oxford: The University Press, 1932 (for 1930).

Smith, William, ed., *Dictionary of Greek and Roman Biography and Mythology*, 3 vols. London: James Walton, M.DCCC.LXIX.

Spencer, Theodore and Van Doren, Mark, *Studies in Metaphysical Poetry, Two Essays and a Bibliography*. "Richard Crashaw" (A Bibliography). New York: Columbia University Press, Mdcccxxxix.

[Wigram, George V.], *The Englishman's Greek Concordance to the New Testament*. New York: Harper & Bros., 1869.

Wing, Donald, *Short Title Catalogue of Books Printed in England, Scotland, Ireland, Wales, and British America and of English Books Printed in Other Countries 1641-1700*, 3 vols. [The Index Society]. New York: Columbia University Press, 1945.

Young, Robert, *Analytical Concordance to the Bible*, 22nd Amer. edit., revised by Wm. B. Stevenson, and including Index Lexicons to the Old and New Testaments. New York: Funk & Wagnalls, n.d.

INDICES

IMAGES AND SYMBOLS

CRASHAW'S POEMS

CITED IN TEXT AND FOOTNOTES

[First lines and titles (adapted from Martin's Index, pp. 475-476) are given with cross references. The number in parentheses designates the page in Martin on which the poem begins; two such numbers designate beginning pages of the two English versions of the same poem. Translations of the Latin hymns are indexed under the Latin name.]